Level 3 • Book 2

Money
•
Storytelling
•
Country Life

SRA OPEN COURT READING

Level 3 • Book 2

— PROGRAM AUTHORS —

Marilyn Jager Adams	Iva Carruthers	Marsha Roit
Carl Bereiter	Jan Hirshberg	Marlene Scardamalia
Joe Campione	Anne McKeough	Gerald H. Treadway, Jr.
	Michael Pressley	

SRA

A Division of The McGraw·Hill Companies

Columbus, Ohio

Acknowledgments

Grateful acknowledgment is given to the following publishers and copyright owners for permissions granted to reprint selections from their publications. All possible care has been taken to trace ownership and secure permission for each selection included. In case of any errors or omissions, the Publisher will be pleased to make suitable acknowledgements in future editions.

A NEW COAT FOR ANNA by Harriet Ziefert. Text copyright © 1986 by Harriet Ziefert. Illustrations copyright © 1986 by Anita Lobel. Published by arrangement with Random House Children's Books a division of Random House, Inc., New York, New York. All rights reserved.

From ALEXANDER, WHO USED TO BE RICH LAST SUNDAY. Text copyright © 1978 by Judith Viorst, illustrations copyright © 1978 by Ray Cruz. Reprinted with permission of Atheneum Books for Young Readers, Simon & Schuster Children's Publishing Division. All rights reserved.

"Smart" from WHERE THE SIDEWALK ENDS by Shel Silverstein. COPYRIGHT © 1974 BY EVIL EYE MUSIC, INC. Used by permission of HarperCollins Publishers.

"Tony and the Quarter" from ROLLING HARVEY DOWN THE HILL TEXT COPYRIGHT © 1985 BY JACK PRELUTSKY. Used by permission of HarperCollins Publishers.

"Kids Did It! in Business" from WORLD Magazine, June 1996. Judith E. Rinard/National Geographic Image collection.

From THE COBBLER'S SONG by Marcia Sewall, copyright © 1982 by Marcia Sewall. Used by permission of Dutton Children's Books, an imprint of Penguin Putnam Books for Young Readers, a division of Penguin Putnam Inc.

FOUR DOLLARS AND FIFTY CENTS by Eric A. Kimmel. Text copyright © 1989 by Eric A. Kimmel. Illustrations copyright © 1989 by Glen Rounds. All rights reserved. Reprinted by permission of Holiday House, Inc.

From THE GO-AROUND DOLLAR. Text copyright © 1992 by Barbara Johnston Adams, illustrations copyright © 1992 by Joyce Audy Zarins. Reprinted with permission of Simon & Schuster Books for Young Readers, Simon & Schuster Children's Publishing Division. All rights reserved.

From UNCLE JED'S BARBER SHOP. Text copyright © 1993 by Margaree King Mitchell, illustrations copyright © 1993 by James Ransome. Reprinted with permission of Simon & Schuster Books for Young Readers, Simon & Schuster Children's Publishing Division. All rights reserved.

From A STORY, A STORY. Copyright © 1970 by Gail E. Haley. Reprinted with permission of Atheneum Books for Young Readers, Simon & Schuster Children's Publishing Division. All rights reserved.

"Worlds I Know" by Myra Cohn Livingston. Reprinted with the permission of Margaret K. McElderry Books, an imprint of Simon & Schuster Children's Publishing Division from WORLDS I KNOW AND OTHER POEMS by Myra Cohn Livingston. Text copyright © 1985 Myra Cohn Livingston.

STORM IN THE NIGHT by Mary Stolz. TEXT COPYRIGHT © 1988 BY MARY STOLZ, ILLUSTRATIONS COPYRIGHT © 1988 BY PAT CUMMINGS. Used by permission of HarperCollins Publishers.

"Past" from ALL COLORS OF THE RACE BY ARNOLD ADOFF. COPYRIGHT © 1982 BY ARNOLD ADOFF. Used by permission of HarperCollins Publishers.

"Carving the Pole" from TOTEM POLE by Diane Hoyt-Goldsmith. Text copyright © 1990 by Diane Hoyt-Goldsmith. All rights reserved. Photographs copyright © 1990 by Lawrence Migdale. All rights reserved. Reprinted from TOTEM POLE by permission of Holiday House Inc.

From THE KEEPING QUILT: 10th ANNIVERSARY EDITION by Patricia Polacco. Copyright © 1998, by Patricia Polacco. Reprinted with permission of Simon & Schuster Books For Young Readers, Simon & Schuster Children's Publishing Division. All rights reserved.

"Aunt Sue's Stories" from COLLECTED POEMS by Langston Hughes Copyright © 1994 by the Estate of Langston Hughes. Reprinted by permission of Alfred A Knopf, a Division of Random House Inc.

JOHNNY APPLESEED by Steven Kellogg. COPYRIGHT 1988 BY STEVEN KELLOGG. Used by permission of HarperCollins Publishers.

AUNT FLOSSIE'S HATS (AND CRAB CAKES LATER) by Elizabeth Fitzgerald Howard. Text copyright © 1991 by Elizabeth Fitzgerald Howard. Illustrations copyright © 1991 by James Ransome. Reprinted by permission of Clarion Books/Houghton Mifflin Co. All rights reserved.

"Lemon Tree" by Jennifer Clement from THE TREE IS OLDER THAN YOU ARE selected by Naomi Shihab Nye, translated by Consuelo de Aerenlund, copyright © 1995, Simon & Schuster Books for Young Readers. Used by permission of the author.

"The Country Mouse and the City Mouse, text", from AESOP'S FABLES by Heidi Holder, illustrator, copyright © 1981 by Viking Penguin, Inc. Used by permission of Viking Penguin, an imprint of Penguin Putnam Books for Young Readers, a division of Penguin Putnam Inc. "The Country Mouse and the City Mouse, illus." by Heidi Holder from AESOP'S FABLES by Heidi Holder, illustrator, copyright © 1981 by Heidi Holder, illustrations. Used by permission of Viking Penguin, an imprint of Penguin Putnam Books for Young Readers, a division of Penguin Putnam Inc.

HEARTLAND by Diane Siebert. TEXT COPYRIGHT © 1989 BY DIANE SIEBERT. ILLUSTRATIONS COPYRIGHT © 1989 BY WENDELL MINOR. Used by permission of HarperCollins Publishers.

"Rudolph Is Tired of the City" from BRONZEVILLE BOYS AND GIRLS by Gwendolyn Brooks. COPYRIGHT © 1956 BY GWENDOLYN BROOKS BLAKELY. Used by permission of HarperCollins Publishers.

LEAH'S PONY by Elizabeth Friedrich. Text copyright © 1996 by Elizabeth Friedrich. Illustrations copyright © 1996 by Michael Garland from Leah's Pony. Published by Boyds Mills Press, Inc. Reprinted by permission.

From COWS IN THE PARLOR by Cynthia McFarland. Copyright © 1990 Cynthia McFarland. Reprinted with permission of copyright holder.

"Farmworkers" from GATHERING THE SUN by Alma Flor Ada. TEXT COPYRIGHT © 1997 BY ALMA FLOR ADA. ILLUSTRATIONS COPYRIGHT © 1997 BY SIMON SILVA. Translated from the Spanish by Rosa Zubizarreta. Text copyright © 1997 by Alma Flor Ada. Illustrations copyright © 1997 by Simon Silva. Used by permission of HarperCollins Publishers.

"Thanks" from GATHERING THE SUN by Alma Flor Ada. TEXT COPYRIGHT © 1997 BY ALMA FLOR ADA. ILLUSTRATIONS COPYRIGHT © 1997 BY SIMON SILVA. Translated from the Spanish by Rosa Zubizarreta. Text copyright © 1997 by Alma Flor Ada. Illustrations copyright © 1997 by Simon Silva. Used by permission of HarperCollins Publishers.

JUST PLAIN FANCY, Text and illustrations copyright © 1990 by Patricia Polacco. Published by arrangement with Random House Children's Books, a division of Random House, Inc., New York, New York, U.S.A. All rights reserved.

WHAT EVER HAPPENED TO THE BAXTER PLACE? By Pat Ross. Text copyright © 1976 by Pat Ross. Reprinted with permission of the author. Text copyright © 1976 by Pat Ross. Illustrations copyright © 1976 by Roger Duvoisin. Reprinted by arrangement with Jeanne C. Duvoisin, trustee.

Text and images from IF YOU'RE NOT FROM THE PRAIRIE...reprinted with permission of the author, David Bouchard, and the illustrator, Henry Ripplinger. First published in 1993 by Raincoast Books, Vancouver, British Columbia. Text © David Bouchard, 1993. Artwork © Henry Ripplinger, 1993.

www.sra4kids.com

SRA/McGraw-Hill

A Division of The McGraw·Hill Companies

— PROGRAM AUTHORS —

Marilyn Jager Adams, Ph.D.
BBN Technologies

Carl Bereiter, Ph.D.
University of Toronto

Joe Campione, Ph.D.
University of California at Berkeley

Iva Carruthers, Ph.D.
Northeastern Illinois University

Jan Hirshberg, Ed.D.
Reading Specialist

Anne McKeough, Ph.D.
University of Calgary

Michael Pressley, Ph.D.
University of Notre Dame

Marsha Roit, Ph.D.
National Reading Consultant

Marlene Scardamalia, Ph.D.
University of Toronto

Gerald H. Treadway, Jr., Ed.D.
San Diego State University

Table of Contents

Storytelling

9

UNIT 6

Table of Contents

Country Life

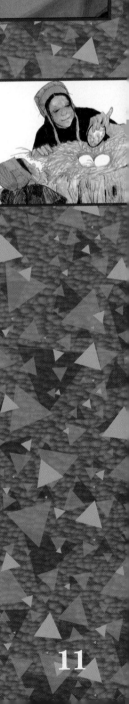

UNIT 4 Money

Everyone likes money. Where did money come from? Who invented it? Why is it so important? There was a time when there was no money. What would it be like if there were no money?

THANKS.

IT'S FRESH!

LEMON. ADE 10¢

13

Focus Questions Why do we sometimes have to give up something we have in order to get something we want? Why are things we receive more special when others have had to work together in order to give them to us?

A New Coat for Anna

Harriet Ziefert
illustrated by Anita Lobel

Winter had come and Anna needed a new coat. The fuzzy blue coat that she had worn for so many winters was no longer fuzzy and it was very small.

Last winter Anna's mother had said, "When the war is over, we will be able to buy things again and I will get you a nice new coat."

But when the war ended the stores remained empty. There still were no coats. There was hardly any food. And no one had any money.

Anna's mother wondered how she could get Anna a new coat. Then she had an idea. "Anna, I have no money," she said, "but I still have Grandfather's gold watch and some other nice things. Maybe we can use them to get what we need for a new coat. First we need wool. Tomorrow we will visit a farmer and see about getting some."

The next day Anna and her mother walked to a nearby farm.

"Anna needs a new coat," Anna's mother told the farmer. "I have no money, but I will give you this fine gold watch if you will give me enough wool from your sheep to make a coat."

The farmer said, "What a good idea! But you will have to wait until spring when I shear my sheep's winter wool. Then I can trade you their wool for your gold watch."

Anna waited for spring to come. Almost every Sunday she and her mother visited the sheep. She would always ask them, "Is your wool growing?" The sheep would always answer, "Baaa!" Then she would feed them nice fresh hay and give them hugs.

At Christmastime Anna brought them paper necklaces and apples and sang carols.

When spring came the farmer sheared the sheep's wool.

"Does it hurt them?" asked Anna.

"No, Anna," said the farmer. "It is just like getting a haircut."

When he had enough wool to make a coat, the farmer showed Anna how to card the wool. "It's like untangling the knots in your hair," he told Anna.

Then he gave Anna's mother a big bag of wool and Anna's mother gave him the gold watch.

Anna and her mother took the bag of wool to an old woman who had a spinning wheel.

"Anna needs a new coat," Anna's mother told the woman. "I have no money, but I will give you this beautiful lamp if you will spin this wool into yarn."

The woman said, "A lamp. That's just what I need. But I cannot spin quickly, for I am old and my fingers are stiff. Come back when the cherries are ripe and I will have your yarn."

When summer came, Anna and her mother returned. Anna's mother gave the old woman the lamp and the old woman gave them the yarn—and a basket of delicious red cherries.

"Anna, what color coat would you like?" Anna's mother asked.

"A red one!" Anna answered.

"Then we will pick some lingonberries," said Anna's mother. "They make a beautiful red dye."

At the end of the summer, Anna's mother knew just the place in the woods to find the ripest lingonberries.

Anna and her mother boiled water in a big pot and put the berries into it. The water turned a deep red. Anna's mother dipped the pale yarn into it.

Soon red yarn was hanging up to dry on a clothesline strung across the kitchen.

When it dried, Anna and her mother wound the yarn into balls.

They took the yarn to the weaver.

"Anna needs a new coat," Anna's mother said. "I have no money, but I will give you this garnet necklace if you will weave this yarn into cloth."

The weaver said, "What a pretty necklace. I will be happy to weave your yarn. Come back in two weeks."

When Anna and her mother returned, the weaver gave them a bolt of beautiful red cloth. Anna's mother gave the weaver the sparkling garnet necklace.

The next day Anna and her mother set off to see the tailor.

"Winter is coming and Anna needs a new coat," Anna's mother told the tailor. "I have no money, but I will give you this porcelain teapot if you will make a coat from this cloth."

The tailor said, "That's a pretty teapot. Anna, I'd be very happy to make you a new coat, but first I must take your measurements."

He measured her shoulders. He measured her arms.
He measured from the back of her neck to the back of
her knees. Then he said, "Come back next week and I will
have your coat."

The tailor set to work making a pattern, cutting the
cloth, pinning, and sewing and stitching and snipping.
He worked and worked for almost a whole week. When
he was finished, he found six pretty matching buttons
in his button box and sewed them on the coat.

He hung the coat proudly in the window for everyone
to see.

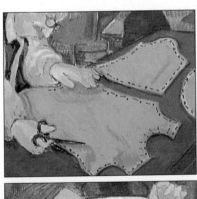

21

When Anna and her mother returned to the tailor's shop, Anna tried on her new coat. She twirled around in front of the mirror. The coat was perfect!

Anna thanked the tailor. Anna's mother thanked him, too, and gave him the pretty porcelain teapot.

Anna wore her new coat home. She stopped at every store to look at her reflection in the window.

When they got home her mother said, "Christmas will soon be here, and I think this year we could have a little celebration."

Anna said, "Oh, yes, and please could we invite all the people who helped to make my coat?"

"Yes," said Anna's mother. "And I will make a Christmas cake just like I used to."

Anna gave her mother a big hug.

On Christmas Eve the farmer, the spinner, the weaver, and the tailor came to Anna's house. They all thought Anna looked beautiful in her new coat.

The Christmas cake that Anna's mother baked was delicious. Everyone agreed that this was the best Christmas they had had in a long time.

On Christmas Day Anna visited the sheep. "Thank you for the wool, sheep," she said. "Do you like my pretty new coat?"

The sheep seemed to smile as they answered, "Baaa! Baaa!"

A New Coat for Anna

Meet the Author

Harriet Ziefert was a schoolteacher for many years. She began looking for jobs as an editor but found that getting hired was tough. So she began writing books. She has written many books—several hundred. She likes to develop a story together with an illustrator. *"I like to work with artists and turn them into illustrators. I like finding new artists and watching them grow."*

Meet the Illustrator

Anita Lobel was born in Poland and grew up during World War II. She became a very successful children's book author and illustrator. Lobel's knowledge of the theater is very important in her work as an illustrator. *"Writing and illustrating books for children is a form of drama for me. I approach the construction of a picture book as if it were a theater piece to be performed, assigning dialogue, dressing the characters, and putting them into an appropriate setting."*

Theme Connections

Within the Selection

Record your answers to the questions below in the Response Journal section of your Writer's Notebook. In small groups, report the ideas you wrote. Discuss your ideas with the rest of the group. Then choose a person to report your group's answers to the class.

- How was Anna's mother able to get Anna a new coat without any money?
- Why do you think Anna's new coat was valuable?

Beyond the Selection

- Have you ever traded with a friend for something you wanted? What did you give in trade?
- Think about what "A New Coat for Anna" tells you about money.
- Add items to the Concept/Question Board about money.

Alexander,
Who Used to Be Rich Last Sunday

Judith Viorst
illustrated by Ray Cruz

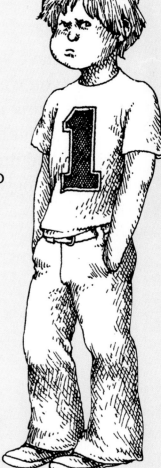

It isn't fair that my brother Anthony has two dollars and three quarters and one dime and seven nickels and eighteen pennies.

It isn't fair that my brother Nicholas has one dollar and two quarters and five dimes and five nickels and thirteen pennies.

It isn't fair because what I've got is . . . bus tokens.

And most of the time what I've mostly got is . . . bus tokens.

And even when I'm very rich, I know that pretty soon what I'll have is . . . bus tokens.

I know because I used to be rich. Last Sunday.

Last Sunday Grandma Betty and Grandpa Louie came to visit from New Jersey. They brought lox because my father likes to eat lox. They brought plants because my mother likes to grow plants.

They brought a dollar for me and a dollar for Nick and a dollar for Anthony because—Mom says it isn't nice to say this—we like money.

A lot. Especially me.

My father told me to put the dollar away to pay for college.

He was kidding.

Anthony told me to use the dollar to go downtown to a store and buy a new face. Anthony stinks.

Nicky said to take the dollar and bury it in the garden and in a week a dollar tree would grow. Ha ha ha.

Mom said if I really want to buy a walkie-talkie, save my money.

Saving money is hard.

Because last Sunday, when I used to be rich, I went to Pearson's Drug Store and got bubble gum. And after the gum stopped tasting good, I got more gum. And after that gum stopped tasting good, I got more gum. And even though I told my friend David I'd sell him all the gum in my mouth for a nickel, he still wouldn't buy it.

Good-bye fifteen cents.

Last Sunday, when I used to be rich, I bet that I could hold my breath till 300. Anthony won. I bet that I could jump from the top of the stoop and land on my feet. Nicky won.

I bet that I could hide this purple marble in my hand, and my mom would never guess which hand I was hiding it in. I didn't know that moms made children pay.

Good-bye another fifteen cents.

I absolutely was saving the rest of my money. I positively was saving the rest of my money. Except that Eddie called me up and said that he would rent me his snake for an hour. I always wanted to rent his snake for an hour.

Good-bye twelve cents.

Anthony said when I'm ninety-nine I still won't have enough for a walkie-talkie. Nick said I'm too dumb to be let loose. My father said that there are certain words a boy can never say, no matter how ratty and mean his brothers are being. My father fined me five cents each for saying them.

Good-bye dime.

Last Sunday, when I used to be rich, by accident I flushed three cents down the toilet. A nickel fell through a crack when I walked on my hands. I tried to get my nickel out with a butter knife and also my mother's scissors.

Good-bye eight cents.

And the butter knife.

And the scissors.

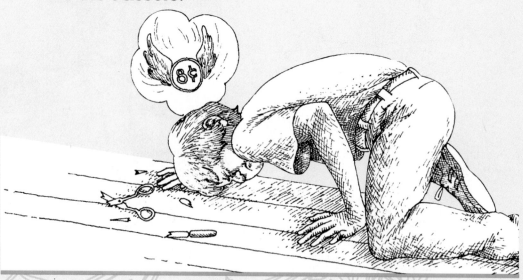

Last Sunday, when I used to be rich, I found
this chocolate candy bar just sitting there. I
rescued it from being melted or smushed. Except
the way I rescued it from being melted or
smushed was that I ate it. How was I supposed to
know it was Anthony's?

Good-bye eleven cents.

I absolutely was saving the rest of my money.
I positively was saving the rest of my money.
But then Nick did a magic trick that made my
pennies vanish in thin air. The trick to bring them
back he hasn't learned yet.

Good-bye four cents.

Anthony said that even when I'm 199, I still won't have enough for a walkie-talkie. Nick said they should lock me in a cage. My father said that there are certain things a boy can never kick, no matter how ratty and mean his brothers are being. My father made me pay five cents for kicking it.

Good-bye nickel.

Last Sunday, when I used to be rich, Cathy around the corner had a garage sale. I positively only went to look. I looked at a half-melted candle. I needed that candle. I looked at a bear with one eye. I needed that bear. I looked at a deck of cards that was perfect except for no seven of clubs and no two of diamonds. I didn't need that seven or that two.

Good-bye twenty cents.

I absolutely was saving the rest of my money. I positively was saving the rest of my money. I absolutely positively was saving the rest of my money. Except I needed to get some money to save.

I tried to make a tooth fall out—I could put it under my pillow and get a quarter. No loose teeth.

I looked in Pearson's telephone booths for nickels and dimes that people sometimes forget. No one forgot.

I brought some non-returnable bottles down to Friendly's Market. Friendly's Market wasn't very friendly.

I told my grandma and grandpa to come back soon.

Last Sunday, when I used to be rich, I used to have a dollar. I do not have a dollar any more. I've got this dopey deck of cards. I've got this one-eyed bear. I've got this melted candle.

And . . . some bus tokens.

Alexander,
Who Used to Be Rich Last Sunday

Meet the Author

Judith Viorst writes almost all of her children's stories about her sons and their adventures. *"I find my sons fierce and funny,"* she says, *"and these qualities appear in many of my characters, some of whom are named after my boys."* Judith wrote poems and stories as a child, and when she was older, she kept writing. She has also written books with her husband and has had her own column in a magazine.

Meet the Illustrator

Ray Cruz was born and raised in New York City. He went to an art and design school during his high school years and then went on to study art in college. Being an illustrator has allowed him to work in many different types of jobs. He has worked for advertising agencies, cosmetic companies, textile companies, and of course, publishing companies. Besides illustration, his interests are art history, archaeology, and conservation.

Theme Connections

Within the Selection

Record your answers to the questions below in the Response Journal section of your Writer's Notebook. In small groups, report the ideas you wrote. Discuss your ideas with the rest of the group. Then choose a person to report your group's answers to the class.

- How did having money cause a problem for Alexander?
- Why was it so hard for Alexander to save his money?

Across Selections

- How is Alexander's problem different than Anna's and her mother's?

Beyond the Selection

- Is it important to be wise about the way you use your money? Why?
- Think about how "Alexander, Who Used to Be Rich Last Sunday" adds to what you know about money.
- Add items to the Concept/Question Board about money.

Smart

Shel Silverstein

My dad gave me one dollar bill
'Cause I'm his smartest son,
And I swapped it for two shiny quarters
'Cause two is more than one!

And then I took the quarters
And traded them to Lou
For three dimes—I guess he don't know
That three is more than two!

Just then, along came old blind Bates
And just 'cause he can't see
He gave me four nickels for my three dimes,
And four is more than three!

And I took the nickels to Hiram Coombs
Down at the seed-feed store,
And the fool gave me five pennies for them,
And five is more than four!

And then I went and showed my dad,
And he got red in the cheeks
And closed his eyes and shook his head—
Too proud of me to speak!

Tony and the Quarter

Jack Prelutsky • *illustrated by Victoria Chess*

Tony's my neighbor
and Tony's my friend.
Today Tony's ma
gave him money to spend.

He slapped my behind
and he said with a laugh,
"Whatever I get,
you can have almost half.

I got a whole quarter,
I'll split it with you.
Let's go get some candy
and bubble gum too."

So happily downhill
the two of us tore,
to see what a quarter
would buy at the store.

But things didn't work
just the way that we planned,
Tony tripped—and the quarter
flew out of his hand.

It rolled down the sidewalk
and oh, what a pain!
We couldn't catch up
and it went down the drain.

Such a dumb thing to do,
oh, it made me so sore.
Still, I guess I like Tony
as much as before.

Focus Questions What would it be like to own your own business? What do you think you would need to start a business? What characteristics are important in running a successful business?

Kids Did It!
in Business

by Judith E. Rinard

The Bug Buster

Adam Baratz, 10

Is something bugging your computer? Meet Adam Baratz. Bugs are his business—computer bugs, that is. For years, Adam, who lives in Newton, Massachusetts, has been catching those pesky "bugs," mistakes or glitches in computer software programs that can make computers malfunction.

A computer user since he was 2 years old, Adam found his first bug at age 5. Today he tests software programs for big companies such as Microsoft. Program testers like Adam are called beta (BAY-tuh) testers. They try out beta, or second, versions of new programs. The third version is released to the public. Companies use thousands of beta testers. But Adam, who started testing when he was 8, may be the youngest.

How does Adam test for bugs? "I play around with the program to see what it can do," he says. "I feel like a detective. You have to work hard to track down bugs or they can really mess up your computer." Adam gets paid for his skills with free copies of the programs. "The best part is that I get to look at the programs before anyone else," he says. Adam has also written newspaper columns reviewing educational software for kids. Adam enjoys his job. "It's fun," he says. "I just really like computers!"

Fashioning a Success

Ebony Hood, 18

Minding her own business is fun and profitable for Ebony Hood of Washington, D.C. She's started her own business selling fashion pins and scarves like the ones she's modeling here. Ebony learned how to set up a business, order merchandise, and keep records in a special course at her high school.

Ebony sells her brightly colored fashions at school and in friends' homes. During her first four months in business, she earned nearly $1,000.

"I love being in charge, being my own boss, and dealing with people," says Ebony. Now she's added a new business: baking fancy cakes and catering parties. What's her most challenging catering task? "Not breaking the cakes!"

Ebony plans to use her earnings for college. To succeed in business, she advises, requires "honesty, a good personality, and hard work."

Greetings!

Marc Wright, 10

When Marc Wright lays his cards on the table, he has quite a few. Marc owns his own greeting card company, called Kiddie Cards. He started the company four years ago when he was just 6. "I wanted to make extra money," says Marc of Windsor, Ontario, in Canada. "One day I drew a picture. My mom suggested I put it on a greeting card." Marc did, and his company was launched.

At first Marc made and sold his own cards, going door to door. The cards really caught on, and people wanted more. "So I hired friends to help," he says. About 20 young artists ages 5 to 13 now work for Marc. He pays them 25 cents a card and sells the cards for about $1. He donates 10 percent of his profits to a children's charity.

Marc's business has earned up to $3,000 a year and now includes mail orders worldwide. The best part of the business? "Being able to do things like take my mom on a vacation to Walt Disney World," says Marc.

A Sizzling Idea

Abbey Fleck, 12

Abbey Fleck of St. Paul, Minnesota, really knows how to bring home the bacon. In fact, when she was 8, she invented a gadget that does just that! Called "Makin' Bacon," her invention is a plastic dish with T-shaped bars. You hang bacon over the bars to cook in the microwave oven. The fat drips off the bacon as it cooks, producing a crisper, healthier bacon with less mess. Abbey's invention is now her family's business. How did Abbey think of it? "I was watching my dad cook bacon one morning," says Abbey. "When he ran out of paper towels to drain the grease, I said, 'Why not just hang it up while it's cooking?'" Abbey and her dad designed and perfected "Makin' Bacon." Now it's widely sold. "I'm proud I thought of it," says Abbey. "And it's neat to know my idea is now supporting my family!"

Kids Did It!
in Business

Meet the Author

Judith E. Rinard writes for the National Geographic Society. Besides writing, she loves drawing, painting, traveling, and camping. Most of her writing is about nature and foreign cultures.

Theme Connections

Within the Selection

Record your answers to the questions below in the Response Journal section of your Writer's Notebook. In small groups, report the ideas you wrote. Discuss your ideas with the rest of the group. Then choose a person to report your group's answers to the class.

- What do all of the children in this article have in common?
- What kinds of things do the children do with the money they earn?

Across Selections

- How is Adam's business similar to the way in which Anna and her mother conduct business?

Beyond the Selection

- What type of business could you and your friends start?
- Think about how "Kids Did It! in Business" adds to what you know about money.
- Add items to the Concept/Question Board about money.

The Cobbler's Song

a fable by Jean de La Fontaine

adapted and illustrated by Marcia Sewall

Once upon a time a poor cobbler lived in the basement of a large house in Paris. He had to work from early morning until late at night to make enough money to keep himself and his wife and children. But he was happy in his dark little rooms, and he sang all day as he mended old shoes.

On the floor above him lived a very rich man. His rooms were large and sunny. He wore fine clothes and had plenty of good things to eat. Still, he was never happy.

All night long he lay awake thinking about his money——how to make more, or fearing lest it be stolen. Often the sun was shining in at his windows before he fell asleep.

Now, as soon as it grew light enough to see, the cobbler always got up and went about his work. And as he hammered, he sang. His songs floated up to the rooms of the rich man and woke him.

"This is just dreadful!" said the rich man. "I cannot sleep at night for thinking of my money, and I cannot sleep in the daytime because of the singing of that silly cobbler."

So the rich man sat down and thought the matter over.

"Hmm," he said to himself, "if the cobbler had something to worry about, he would not sing so much. I must think of a plan to stop him. Let me see, what worries men most?

"Why money, to be sure! Some men worry because they have so little. The cobbler has little enough, it's true, but that does not worry him. In fact, he is the happiest man I know.

"Other men worry because they have too much money, which is my trouble. I wonder if it would worry the cobbler if he had too much. That's the idea! Now I know what I shall do!"

A few minutes later, the rich man entered the cobbler's poor home.

"What can I do for you?" asked the cobbler, recognizing his neighbor but wondering why so fine a man should enter his little shop.

"Here, I have brought you a present," said the rich man, and he gave the poor man a purse.

The cobbler opened it and saw that it was full of shining gold pieces.

"I cannot take all this money!" cried he. "I have not earned it. Take it back."

"No," answered the rich man, "you have earned it by your songs. I give it to you because you are the happiest man I know."

Without waiting for any thanks, the rich man left the shop.

The cobbler turned the gold pieces out on his table and began to count them. He had counted to fifty-two, when he looked up and saw a man passing by the window. He quickly hid the gold. Then he went into the bedroom to count it where no one could see him.

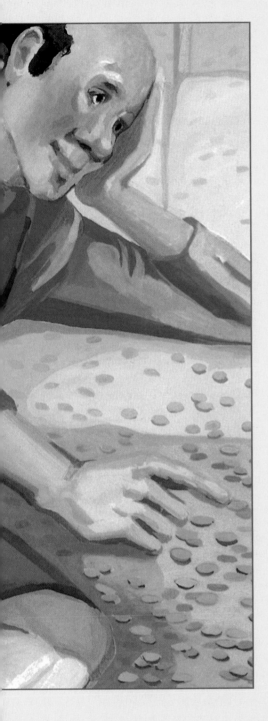

He piled the coins up on the bed. How golden they were! How bright! He had never seen so much money before. He looked and looked at the money until everything in the room seemed golden and bright. Then he counted it slowly.

"One hundred pieces of gold! How rich I am! Where shall I hide it for safekeeping?"

First he hid the coins under the covers at the foot of the bed, which he could see from his workbench.

"The money makes quite a lump under the covers," he said. "Perhaps someone else will see it and steal it. I think I should hide it under the pillow."

While he was putting it under the pillow, his wife came into the room.

"What is the matter with the bed?" she asked.

The cobbler glared at her, and drove her from the room with angry words——the first cross words he had ever spoken to her.

Dinner came, but he could not eat a mouthful because he was afraid someone would steal his treasure while he was at the table! As he worked, not a note did he sing. By suppertime he felt worse. Not a kind word did he speak to his wife.

Day after day and night after night, the cobbler grew more and more unhappy, worrying about his money. He dared not go to sleep, lest he should wake to find that his gold had disappeared. He tossed and turned on his pillow.

But upstairs, the rich man was happy. "That was a fine idea," he said to himself drowsily. "Now I can sleep all day without being awakened by the cobbler's song."

For a month, the cobbler worried over the hundred gold pieces. He grew thin and pale, and his wife and children were most unhappy. At last he could bear the worry no longer, so he called his wife and told her the whole story.

"Dear husband," she said, "take back the gold. All the gold in the world is not worth as much to me as your happiness and one of your glad songs."

How relieved the cobbler felt to hear her say this. He picked up the purse and ran upstairs to the rich man's home. Throwing the gold on the table, he smiled and said: "Here is your purse of gold. Take it back! I can live without your money, but I cannot live without my song."

The Cobbler's Song

Meet the Author

Jean de La Fontaine was born in France in 1621. He is best known for his collection of nearly 250 fables. In six volumes of writing, he took existing fables, built on them, and turned them into poetry. His writings about everyday life and the choices people face have remained popular for more than 350 years.

Meet the Illustrator

Marcia Sewall adapted and illustrated this fable written by Jean de La Fontaine. Her home and family have been very influential in her life and career. *"The interests of my family have come together in my own desire to illustrate books. My father was full of good tales, particularly of Maine, and would love to entertain us with long humorous poems memorized, and anecdotes [stories] of people. My mother has always been artistic in so many different ways."*

Theme Connections

Within the Selection

Record your answers to the questions below in the Response Journal section of your Writer's Notebook. In small groups, report the ideas you wrote. Discuss your ideas with the rest of the group. Then choose a person to report your group's answers to the class.

- How did money affect the rich man and the cobbler?
- Why did the cobbler give the gold back to the rich man?

Across Selections

- What did the cobbler have in common with Anna and her mother?
- What other story have you read in which money has caused a problem?

Beyond the Selection

- Think about how "The Cobbler's Song" adds to what you know about money.
- Add items to the Concept/Question Board about money.

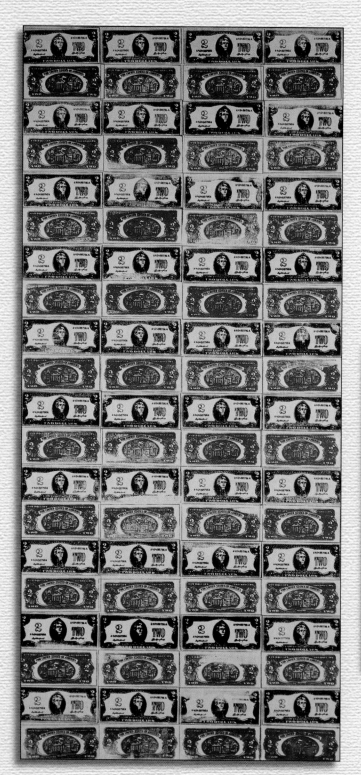

80 Two-Dollar Bills (front and rear).
1962. **Andy Warhol.** Silkscreen on canvas.
Museum Ludwig, Cologne, Germany.
©2001 The Andy Warhol Foundation for
the Visual Arts/Artist Rights Society
(ARS), New York.

*Daric coin, first minted under
Darius I of Persia.* 4th century B.C.
Gold. Diameter: $\frac{9}{16}$". Ashmolean Museum,
Oxford, England.

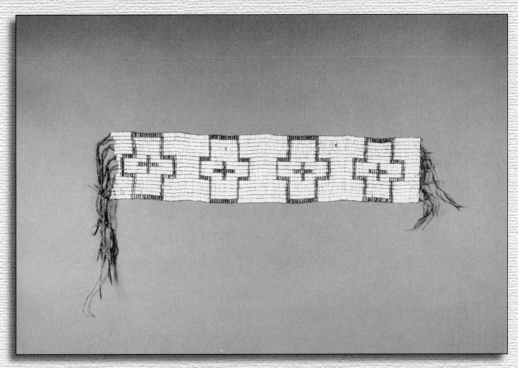

Four Dollars and Fifty Cents

Eric A. Kimmel
illustrated by Glen Rounds

It's a terrible thing to call a cowboy a deadbeat,
but in Shorty Long's case it was true. He owed
everybody money, from Big Oscar the
blacksmith to Widow Macrae, who ran the Silver
Dollar Cafe and baked the best biscuits west of
the Rockies.

"Shorty ain't a bad sort. He just hates to pay for
anything he thinks he can get free," Big Oscar
told the widow one afternoon over coffee at the
Silver Dollar.

The widow brought Oscar another plate of
biscuits. "How am I gonna keep this place going
if folks won't pay their bills? Shorty's the worst.
He owes me four dollars and fifty cents."

Big Oscar shook his head. "You got as much
chance of collecting that money as seeing Custer
ride back from the Little Bighorn."

Widow Macrae picked up her rolling pin.
"That's what you think. I'm driving out to the
Circle K this afternoon. If Shorty won't pay what
he owes, I'll lay him out flatter 'n the bottom of a
skillet."

As soon as Oscar left, Widow Macrae hitched her two horses, Clementine and Evangeline, to the buckboard and drove out to the Circle K ranch. Duck Pooley saw her coming. He rode back to the corral to warn Shorty.

"Widow Macrae's coming! She's got a rolling pin in her hand and an awful mean look in her eye. You better come up with that money, Shorty."

"Boys, you gotta help me!" Shorty yelped.

"Why don't you just pay what you owe?"

"It ain't that simple. If I paid the widow back, everybody I owe money to'd expect the same. I'd end up broker 'n a mess of eggs."

The Circle K boys decided to help Shorty out just for the fun of seeing what would happen. They knocked together a few boards to make a coffin. When Widow Macrae drove up, she found Shorty lying in it. He looked real peaceful. The Circle K boys stood around blubbering, wiping their noses on their sleeves.

Widow Macrae got down from the buckboard. "What happened to Shorty?" she asked.

"He's gone to the last roundup," the Circle K boys told her. "A bronco threw him. He landed on his head."

The widow leaned over for a closer look. Shorty looked deader 'n a Christmas tree in August. But she still wasn't sold, although she kept her suspicions to herself.

"Poor Shorty. It hurts my heart to see him like this. Where do you boys figure on burying him?"

"Why, here on the ranch. Somewheres."

Widow Macrae frowned. "That's not right. Shorty deserves better than sagebrush and coyotes. I know you don't have time to spare, what with the spring roundup coming on. But if you let me take Shorty back to town, I'll see he gets a decent burial."

The Circle K boys could hardly refuse.

"Then it's settled. Some of you boys load Shorty onto the buckboard. Try not to bounce him around too much."

"I'll nail the lid down," Duck Pooley volunteered.

"Not just yet," said Widow Macrae. "I want to see him one last time before I put him in the ground. Shorty Long was my friend."

That sure was news to Shorty. He didn't say a word, but he was thinking hard, mostly about what he'd like to do to Duck Pooley.

With the coffin loaded, Widow Macrae headed back towards town. She turned off onto the Boot Hill road. Boot Hill is where they bury cowboys like Shorty, who die with their boots on. It's a mighty rough road for a feller's last journey.

Widow Macrae reined in at the top of the hill next to a freshly dug grave. She got down from the buckboard, unhitched the horses, and turned them loose to graze. Then she took hold of the coffin and dragged it out of the wagon. Shorty saw stars when the coffin hit the ground, but he

was bound and determined not to pay that four dollars and fifty cents, so he lay still.

The widow studied him hard. "Can you hear me, Shorty? If you can, listen good. I don't know if you're dead or not, but I'm gonna keep my eyes on you all night. If you ain't moved by morning, into the ground you go!"

Poor Shorty! It was pay up or be buried alive—and he couldn't make up his mind which was worse! The sun went down. With Widow Macrae's eyes fixed on him tight, Shorty lay still in his coffin, not moving a muscle, not hardly breathing, waiting for something to happen.

On about midnight something did. Riders! He heard them coming up the Boot Hill road. Widow Macrae ducked behind a tombstone. As for Shorty, he was sure it was a posse of dead cowboys riding back from the grave for one last roundup. He lay in his coffin, stiff as rawhide, hoping that with all the graves up there they wouldn't notice one extra corpse.

Three riders reined in at the top of Boot Hill. They got off their horses. One lit a lantern while the other two lugged an iron strongbox over to the open grave. Anyone would recognize them at once. It was Big Nose George Parrott and two of his gang, Smiley Dunlap and the Oregon Kid. The outlaws started bragging about a train they robbed that afternoon. They came to the graveyard to divide the loot. No one would think of looking for outlaws on Boot Hill. Not live ones, anyway.

Shorty was in a heap of trouble. If those outlaws caught him spying on them, he wouldn't

have to worry about being a fake corpse.
Big Nose George drew his six-gun.

"Stand back, boys! I'll settle this business!"

He fired a shot into the strongbox padlock.
Shorty nearly gave up the ghost. He thought
that bullet was meant for him.

"Yahoo! We struck it rich!"

The Oregon Kid kicked open the lid. He and
Smiley reached inside and began throwing
fistfuls of hundred dollar bills into the air. That
made Big Nose George real mad.

"Quit that clowning! This ain't the circus! You
boys pick up them greenbacks and put 'em back
where you found 'em!"

"Aw, George!"

"Aw, George nothing! We're gonna divvy it up business-like. No grabbing!"

The Kid and Smiley started picking up the money. One of the bills landed in Shorty's coffin.

"Holy Hannah! What's this? There's a dead 'un here!"

"Don't drop your britches, boys. Dead 'uns don't bite." Big Nose George moseyed over for a closer look. "Why, it's some poor cowpoke whose burying had to wait till morning. They should've covered him up, though. It ain't decent leaving a feller out in the open where the buzzards can get at him. But that ain't none of our concern. Bring over them bills and let's get started."

"Can't we close that coffin first?" the Kid asked. "Dead 'uns give me the willies."

"Sure, go ahead," said Big Nose George.

The Kid slammed the coffin lid right down on Shorty's nose! Tears came to Shorty's eyes. He clenched his teeth to keep from yelling.

"What's the matter?" Smiley asked.

"This lid don't fit."

"Let me try." Smiley sat down hard on the coffin. He packed a lot of weight. The lid mashed Shorty's nose into his face. Shorty saw stars, but not the ones in the sky.

"What's keeping you two?" Big Nose George growled.

"This lid won't lay flat."

"Let me see." Big Nose George had a look. "Are you both crack-brained? Use your eyes. This feller's nose sticks up a mile. It's way too long for the coffin."

"What'll we do?"

"Easy! He don't need a sniffer where he's going. I'll cut it off with my bowie knife!"

That was enough for Shorty. He sat up in his coffin and hollered, "Hold on, boys! I ain't that dead!"

Big Nose George nearly dropped his teeth.

Smiley let out a yell as the whole gang ran for their horses.

Those outlaws shot out of that graveyard faster than fireworks!

Widow Macrae laughed fit to bust. When she was all laughed out, she came from behind the tombstone and gave Shorty the scolding of his life.

"I hope you learned your lesson. You nearly got your nose cut off for four dollars and fifty cents!"

Shorty was too embarrassed to say anything. He and Widow Macrae gathered up the money the outlaws left behind. In the morning they took it to the railroad agent in town. He gave

them a five-hundred-dollar reward to divide
between them.

Shorty rubbed his nose. "I reckon we're
even now."

"Not quite," said Widow Macrae. "You still owe
me four dollars and fifty cents."

Shorty stared glumly at his pile of fifty-dollar
bills. "I don't have no change. How about if I
come by tomorrow and settle up?"

"I'll expect you," Widow Macrae said.

But so far as anyone knows, he hasn't paid
her yet.

Meet the Author

Eric A. Kimmel loved stories as a child. As he was growing up, his grandmother (who spoke five languages besides English) would tell him wild stories that would go on for days. Her storytelling inspired him to become a great storyteller himself. He also loved books. He remembers how he felt when he first realized that real people wrote the books. *"I felt electrified. I wanted that. I wanted to have my name on the cover of a book. It was the most wonderful thing I could imagine. I still get a shiver of excitement whenever I take a new book out of the envelope and hold it for the first time. Wow, I did that! I wrote a book! It never fails to amaze me."*

Meet the Illustrator

Glen Rounds held many jobs before becoming an author and illustrator. He was a cowboy, sign painter, railroad section hand, baker, carnival medicine man, textile designer, and staff sergeant in the army, among other things. Eventually he went to New York to get into the book business. He wrote more than 50 books and illustrated over 60 other publications by other authors. Although he is classified as a children's author, he insists that his works are meant for all age groups.

Theme Connections

Within the Selection

Record your answers to the questions below in the Response Journal section of your Writer's Notebook. In small groups, report the ideas you wrote. Discuss your ideas with the rest of the group. Then choose a person to report your group's answers to the class.

- Shorty owed people money. What kinds of problems did this cause for him?
- Why could Shorty be called a deadbeat?

Across Selections

- How were Shorty's ideas about paying debts different from Anna's mother's ideas about paying debts?

Beyond the Selection

- Why is it important to pay back money you owe?
- Think about how "Four Dollars and Fifty Cents" adds to what you know about money.
- Add items to the Concept/Question Board about money.

Focus Questions How do you think paper money is made? Who do you think makes paper money? What do you think the symbols on the one-dollar bill represent?

The Go-Around Dollar

Barbara Johnston Adams
illustrated by Joyce Audy Zarins

Every dollar travels from person to person in a different way. But each dollar starts out in the same place—the Bureau of Engraving and Printing in Washington, D.C. Since 1862, this is where our nation's paper money has been produced. The Bureau is part of the United States Treasury Department. At the Bureau, huge printing presses run around the clock, turning out dollar bills. In twenty-four hours, ten million one-dollar bills can be printed.

Dollars are printed in big sheets of thirty-two bills. First the basic design is printed. Then the sheets are cut in half and go back to the presses for an overprinting. This second printing adds information such as the serial numbers and the Treasury seal.

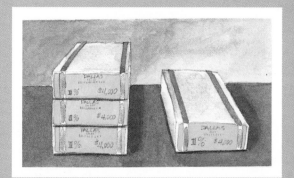

As bills are made, they're checked by people and machines over and over again to make sure they are perfect.

Finally, the sheets are cut into stacks of individual bills called bricks. Bricks are sent to one of twelve banks, located in different parts of the United States, called Federal Reserve Banks. Federal Reserve Banks, in turn, send dollars to banks in cities, small towns, and neighborhoods. From here, dollars go into circulation, to be used by people all over America: in stores, cafeterias, movie theaters, and thousands of other places—wherever money changes hands. Here's what might have happened to one dollar. . . .

The United States government has laws about the way dollar bills can be shown. For instance, a dollar drawn as an illustration for a book must be in black and white, not in full color. A dollar must also be shown either larger than one and one-half times the size of a real dollar, or smaller than three-quarters the size of a real dollar.

73

As Matt and Eric were walking home from school one day . . .

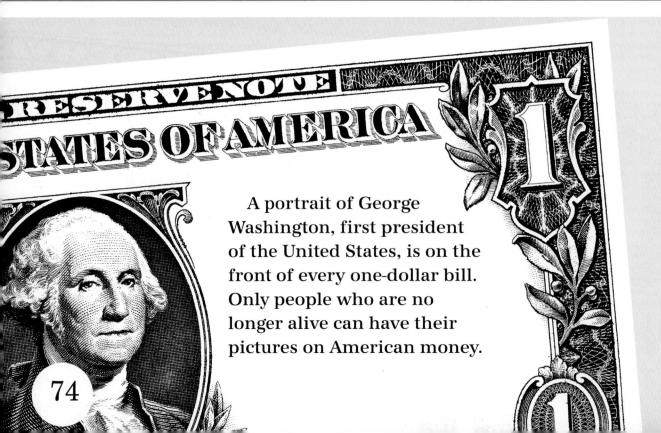

A portrait of George Washington, first president of the United States, is on the front of every one-dollar bill. Only people who are no longer alive can have their pictures on American money.

"What's that?"

"Wow! It's a dollar bill!"

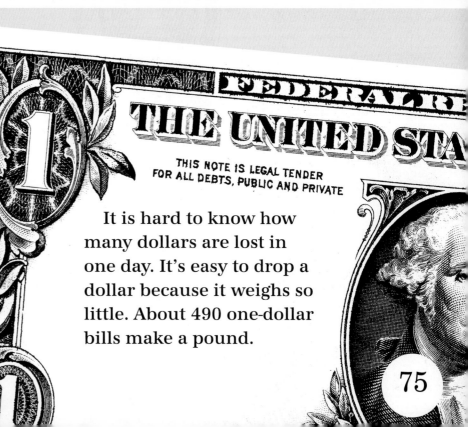

THIS NOTE IS LEGAL TENDER
FOR ALL DEBTS, PUBLIC AND PRIVATE

It is hard to know how many dollars are lost in one day. It's easy to drop a dollar because it weighs so little. About 490 one-dollar bills make a pound.

75

Matt offered to buy Eric's shoelaces for the dollar.

Dollar bills are used to buy things, pay back money that was borrowed, or pay for a service, such as a bus ride. There is a notice on each dollar that makes this clear: "This note is legal tender for all debts, public and private."

SERVE NOTE

TES OF AMERICA

G 90445557 D

The front of every dollar has a long number in green ink, which appears in two different places. This is called the serial number. No two dollars have the same serial number. If a dollar is damaged while it is printed, it is replaced by a bill with a star where the last letter of the serial number would usually be. These bills are called star notes.

SHINGTON

OLLAR

. . . and Jennifer received the dollar as part of her change from a five-dollar bill.

If dollars are in water a short time, they usually aren't damaged. They can't be ripped easily, either. This is because dollars are printed on especially strong paper made of cotton, linen, and silk. If you look closely, you can see the red and blue silk threads.

Jennifer went to a flea market and bought a funny hat from Rob with the dollar. At a booth near Rob's, a ticket seller was handed an odd-looking dollar bill.

The formula for the black and green inks used to print dollars is a secret known only by the Bureau of Engraving and Printing. The secret is important; it keeps people from making fake, or counterfeit, bills exactly like the real ones.

Sometimes people called counterfeiters *do* make fake money. But it's very hard to make a dollar that looks and feels like a real one. When counterfeiters are caught, they're fined and sent to jail.

Back at home, Rob asked his sister Kathy to do a chore for him. . . .

When a dollar changes hands, many people don't realize they're holding the Great Seal of the United States. The two sides of the Seal, an official symbol of our country, are shown in circles on the back of every one-dollar bill. One circle has an eagle in it; the other, a pyramid with an eye. The bald eagle, our national emblem, is holding arrows and an olive branch. The arrows stand for war and the olive branch for peace. The eagle faces the olive branch, which means the United States wants peace, not war. The pyramid stands for strength and growth; the eye, spiritual values.

"Come back here, Biscuit!"

Sometimes dollars are accidentally burned, chewed by animals, or torn. The Treasury Department will replace a bill if more than half of the original remains. If less than half remains, a government official must inspect the dollar before replacing it.

Lots of people say they see pictures of tiny owls or spiders near the corners of dollar bills. But the Bureau of Engraving and Printing says there are no such creatures on our money.

Kathy thought about different ways
to spend the dollar.

One-dollar bills wear out in about eighteen months because they are passed from person to person so often. Banks collect worn-out bills and send them to one of the Federal Reserve Banks. There they are shredded by machine into little pieces too small to be put together again. But once in a while, people will keep a dollar because it has special meaning for them.

The Go-Around Dollar

Meet the Author

Barbara Johnston and her family live in Virginia. She writes nonfiction books for children. She has even written a book about the life of the famous comedian, Bill Cosby. Another book, which she wrote under a different name, is about women who have won the Nobel Prize. Her books have been chosen for the Child Study Association of America's Children's Books of the Year.

Meet the Illustrator

Joyce Audy Zarins has written as well as illustrated children's books. On a regular basis, she illustrates for children's magazines. Readers can find her illustrations in books such as *Log Cabin in the Woods; Toasted Bagels; Sand Dollar, Sand Dollar; Mrs. Peloki's Snake;* and *Piskies, Spriggans, and Other Magical Beings.* Currently, Zarins lives in Massachusetts.

Theme Connections

Within the Selection

Record your answers to the questions below in the Response Journal section of your Writer's Notebook. In small groups, report the ideas you wrote. Discuss your ideas with the rest of the group. Then choose a person to report your group's answers to the class.

- What types of symbols appear on the U. S. one-dollar bill?
- What role does the government play in making and maintaining paper money?

Across Selections

- Compare the way Kathy spent money to the way Alexander in "Alexander, Who Used to Be Rich Last Sunday" spent money.
- In what way is "The Go-Around Dollar" like "A New Coat for Anna"?

Beyond the Selection

- What are some different ways you like to spend money?
- Have you ever saved paper or coin money for a special reason?
- Think about how "The Go-Around Dollar" adds to what you know about money.
- Add items to the Concept/Question Board about money.

Focus Questions What is it like to save for a long time for something you really want? How would you feel if you saved a lot of money for something you wanted and then had to spend it on something else? How would you feel if that something else was very important and your money was going to a good cause?

UNCLE JED'S BARBERSHOP

Margaree King Mitchell

illustrated by James Ransome

Jedediah Johnson was my granddaddy's brother. Everybody has their favorite relative. Well, Uncle Jedediah was mine.

He used to come by our house every Wednesday night with his clippers. He was the only black barber in the county. Daddy said that before Uncle Jed started cutting hair, he and Granddaddy used to have to go thirty miles to get a haircut.

After Uncle Jed cut my daddy's hair, he lathered a short brush with soap and spread it over my daddy's face and shaved him. Then he started over on my granddaddy.

I always asked Uncle Jed to cut my hair, but Mama wouldn't let him. So he would run the clippers on the back of my neck and just pretend to cut my hair. He even spread lotion on my neck. I would smell wonderful all day.

When he was done, he would pick me up and sit me in his lap and tell me about the barbershop he was going to open one day and about all the fancy equipment that would be in it. The sinks would be so shiny they sparkled, the floors so clean you could see yourself. He was going to have four barber chairs. And outside was going to be a big, tall, red-and-white barber pole. He told me he was saving up for it.

He had been saying the same things for years. Nobody believed him. People didn't have dreams like that in those days.

We lived in the South. Most people were poor. My daddy owned a few acres of land and so did a few others. But most people were sharecroppers. That meant they lived in a shack and worked somebody else's land in exchange for a share of the crop.

When I was five years old, I got sick. This particular morning, I didn't come into the kitchen while Mama was fixing breakfast. Mama and Daddy couldn't wake me up. My nightgown and the bedclothes were all wet where I had sweated.

Mama wrapped me in a blanket while Daddy went
outside and hitched the horse to the wagon. We had
to travel about twenty miles into town to the hospital.
It was midday when we got there. We had to go to the
colored waiting room. In those days, they kept blacks
and whites separate. There were separate public rest
rooms, separate water fountains, separate schools. It
was called segregation. So in the hospital, we had to
go to the colored waiting room.

Even though I was unconscious, the doctors
wouldn't look at me until they had finished with all
the white patients. When the doctors did examine me,
they told my daddy that I needed an operation and
that it would cost three hundred dollars.

Three hundred dollars was a lot of money in those days. My daddy didn't have that kind of money. And the doctors wouldn't do the operation until they had the money.

My mama bundled me back up in the blanket and they took me home. Mama held me in her arms all night. She kept me alive until Daddy found Uncle Jed. He found him early the next morning in the next county on his way to cut somebody's hair. Daddy told him about me.

Uncle Jed leaned on his bent cane and stared straight ahead. He told Daddy that the money didn't matter. He couldn't let anything happen to his Sarah Jean.

Well, I had the operation. For a long time after that, Uncle Jed came by the house every day to see how I was doing. I know that three hundred dollars delayed him from opening the barbershop.

Uncle Jed came awfully close to opening his shop a few years after my operation. He had saved enough money to buy the land and build the building. But he still needed money for the equipment.

Anyway, Uncle Jed had come by the house. We had just finished supper when there was a knock on the door. It was Mr. Ernest Walters, a friend of Uncle Jed's. He had come by to tell Uncle Jed about the bank failing. That was where Mr. Walters and Uncle Jed had their money. Uncle Jed had over three thousand dollars in the bank, and it was gone.

Uncle Jed just stood there a long time before he said anything. Then he told Mr. Walters that even though he was disappointed, he would just have to start all over again.

Talk about some hard times. That was the
beginning of the Great Depression. Nobody had
much money.

But Uncle Jed kept going around to his customers
cutting their hair, even though they couldn't pay him.
His customers shared with him whatever they had—a
hot meal, fresh eggs, vegetables from the garden. And
when they were able to pay again, they did.

And Uncle Jed started saving all over again.

Ol' Uncle Jed finally got his barbershop. He opened it on his seventy-ninth birthday. It had everything, just like he said it would—big comfortable chairs, four cutting stations. You name it! The floors were so clean, they sparkled.

On opening day, people came from all over the county. They were Ol' Uncle Jed's customers. He had walked to see them for so many years. That day they all came to him.

I believe he cut hair all night and all the next day and the next night and the day after that! That man was so glad to have that shop, he didn't need any sleep.

Of course, I was there, too. I wouldn't have missed it for the world. When I sat in one of the big barber chairs, Uncle Jed patted the back of my neck with lotion like he always did. Then he twirled me round and round in the barber chair.

Uncle Jed died not long after that, and I think he died a happy man. You see, he made his dream come true even when nobody else believed in it.

He taught me to dream, too.

UNCLE JED'S
BARBERSHOP

Meet the Author

Margaree King Mitchell writes not only children's stories, but television scripts and plays as well. When volunteering at her son's school, she found the inspiration to become a children's book writer. *"I thought if I could somehow write a book that would inspire children to achieve their dreams, then maybe children would be motivated to stay in school and look to the future for a better life for themselves,"* she says. After reading "Uncle Jed's Barbershop" to a group of eight year olds, a girl approached Mitchell to say that she learned she could accomplish everything, even her dream of being a doctor. Mitchell feels that this is the measure of success in writing.

Meet the Illustrator

James Ransome was born in North Carolina. He became interested in art when he was just a child and loved to look at the illustrations in superhero comic books. He was also influenced by television cartoons and *Mad* magazine. Now that he is an illustrator, the characters he draws are all very different and special. James Ransome's characters show the cultural and racial differences that make us who we are. Sometimes James Ransome's illustrations appear on book jackets for young adult books.

Theme Connections

Within the Selection

Record your answers to the questions below in the Response Journal section of your Writer's Notebook. In small groups, report the ideas you wrote. Discuss your ideas with the rest of the group. Then choose a person to report your group's answers to the class.

- Why didn't anyone believe that Uncle Jed could save enough money to open a barbershop?
- Why didn't money matter to Uncle Jed when Sarah Jean needed an operation?
- Why do you think Uncle Jed died a happy man?

Across Selections

- Compare the way Uncle Jed spent money to the way Alexander spent money.
- How was Uncle Jed like the kids in "Kids Did It! in Business"?

Beyond the Selection

- Have you ever worked hard to save money? What did you buy?
- Think about how "Uncle Jed's Barbershop" adds to what you know about money.
- Add items to the Concept/Question Board about money.

Storytelling

Stories can take us on wonderful journeys and introduce us to people and places we might never really get to meet. Do you like to hear stories? Do you like to tell stories? What are your favorite stories?

A Story A Story

*an African tale retold
and illustrated by Gail E. Haley*

Many African tales, whether or not they are about Kwaku Ananse the "Spider man," are called "Spider Stories." This book is about how that came to be.

"Spider stories" tell how small, defenseless men or animals outwit others and succeed against great odds. These stories crossed the Atlantic Ocean in the cruel ships that delivered slaves to the Americas. Their descendants still tell some of these stories today. Ananse has become Anancy in the Caribbean isles, while he survives as "Aunt Nancy" in the southern United States.

At times words and phrases are repeated several times. Storytellers repeat words to make them stronger. For example: "So small, so small, so small," means very, very, very small.

Once, oh small children round my knee, there were no stories on earth to hear. All the stories belonged to Nyame, the Sky God. He kept them in a golden box next to his royal stool.

Ananse, the Spider man, wanted to buy the Sky God's stories. So he spun a web up to the sky.

When the Sky God heard what Ananse wanted, he laughed: "Twe, twe, twe. The price of my stories is that you bring me Osebo the leopard-of-the-terrible-teeth, Mmboro the hornets-who-sting-like-fire, and Mmoatia the fairy-whom-men-never-see."

Ananse bowed and answered: "I shall gladly pay the price."

"Twe, twe, twe," chuckled the Sky God. "How can a weak old man like you, so small, so small, so small, pay my price?"

But Ananse merely climbed down to earth to find the things that the Sky God demanded.

Ananse ran along the jungle path—yiridi, yiridi, yiridi—till he came to Osebo the leopard-of-the-terrible-teeth.

"Oho, Ananse," said the leopard, "you are just in time to be my lunch."

Ananse replied: "As for that, what will happen will happen. But first let us play the binding binding game."

The leopard, who was fond of games, asked: "How is it played?"

"With vine creepers," explained Ananse. "I will bind you by your foot and foot. Then I will untie you, and you can tie me up."

"Very well," growled the leopard, who planned to eat Ananse as soon as it was his turn to bind him.

So Ananse tied the leopard
by his foot
by his foot
by his foot
by his foot, with the vine creeper. Then he said:
"Now, Osebo, you are ready to meet the Sky God."
And he hung the tied leopard in a tree in the jungle.

Next Ananse cut a frond from a banana tree and filled a calabash with water. He crept through the tall grasses, sora, sora, sora, till he came to the nest of Mmboro, the hornets-who-sting-like-fire.

Ananse held the banana leaf over his head as an umbrella. Then he poured some of the water in the calabash over his head.

The rest he emptied over the hornets' nest and cried: "It is raining, raining, raining. Should you not fly into my calabash, so that the rain will not tatter your wings?"

"Thank you. Thank you," hummed the hornets, and they flew into the calabash—fom! Ananse quickly stopped the mouth of the gourd.

"Now, Mmboro, you are ready to meet the Sky God," said Ananse. And he hung the calabash full of hornets onto the tree next to the leopard.

Ananse now carved a little wooden doll holding a bowl. He covered the doll from top to bottom with sticky latex gum. Then he filled the doll's bowl with pounded yams.

He set the little doll at the foot of a flamboyant tree where fairies like to dance. Ananse tied one end of a vine round the doll's head and, holding the other end in his hand, he hid behind a bush.

In a little while, Mmoatia the fairy-whom-no-man-sees came dancing, dancing, dancing, to the foot of the flamboyant tree. There she saw the doll holding the bowl of yams.

Mmoatia said: "Gum baby, I am hungry. May I eat some of your yams?"

Ananse pulled at the vine in his hiding place, so that the doll seemed to nod its head. So the fairy took the bowl from the doll and ate all the yams.

"Thank you, Gum baby," said the fairy. But the doll did not answer.

"Don't you reply when I thank you?" cried the angered fairy. The doll did not stir.

"Gum baby, I'll slap your crying place unless you answer me," shouted the fairy. But the wooden doll remained still and silent. So the fairy slapped her crying place—pa! Her hand stuck fast to the gum baby's sticky cheek.

"Let go of my hand, or I'll slap you again."—Pa! She slapped the doll's crying place with her other hand. Now the fairy was stuck to the gum baby with both hands, and she was furious. She pushed against the doll with her feet, and they also stuck fast.

Now Ananse came out of hiding. "You are ready to meet the Sky God, Mmoatia." And he carried her to the tree where the leopard and the hornets were waiting.

Ananse spun a web round Osebo, Mmboro, and Mmoatia. Then he spun a web to the sky. He pulled up his captives behind him, and set them down at the feet of the Sky God.

"O, Nyame," said Ananse, bowing low, "here is the price you ask for your stories: Osebo the leopard-of-the-terrible-teeth, Mmboro the hornets-who-sting-like-fire, and Mmoatia the fairy-whom-men-never-see."

Nyame the Sky God called together all the nobles of his court and addressed them in a loud voice: "Little Ananse, the Spider man, has paid me the price I ask for my stories. Sing his praise. I command you."

"From this day and going on forever," proclaimed the Sky God, "my stories belong to Ananse and shall be called 'Spider Stories.' "

"Eeeee, Eeeee, Eeeee," shouted all the assembled nobles.

So Ananse took the golden box of stories back to earth, to the people of his village. And when he opened the box all the stories scattered to the corners of the world, including this one.

This is my story which I have related. If it be sweet, or if it be not sweet, take some elsewhere, and let some come back to me.

A Story A Story

Meet the Author and Illustrator

Gail Haley became interested in storytelling and creating art when she was still a child. For the first nine years of her life, she was an only child. That gave her plenty of time to entertain herself with stories that she made up as she played along the banks of the Catawba River in North Carolina. As she grew older, her interest in storytelling continued. She went on to write and illustrate her stories. Her interests have included costuming, puppetry, and creating dollhouse-size miniatures, all of which she has used to help her tell stories to children.

Theme Connections

Within the Selection

Record your answers to the questions below in the Response Journal section of your Writer's Notebook. In small groups, report the ideas you wrote. Discuss your ideas with the rest of the group. Then choose a person to report your group's answers to the class.

- "A Story A Story" is a folktale. In a folktale, there is usually a hero or a heroine who has an important goal. Who was the hero in this story? What was his goal?
- What things did the hero in this story have to do before he reached his goal?
- How does this story try to explain the tradition of storytelling?

Beyond the Selection

- Think about what "A Story A Story" tells you about storytelling.
- Add items to the Concept/Question Board about storytelling.

Focus Questions Where is your favorite place to read stories?
How many places in the world can you travel to in
your mind while reading a story or a poem?

Worlds I Know

Myra Cohn Livingston
illustrated by Delana Bettoli

I can read the pictures by myself
in the books that lie on the lowest shelf.
I know the place where the stories start
and some I can even say by heart,
and I make up adventures and dreams and words
for some of the pages I've never heard.

118

But I like it best when Mother sits
and reads to me my favorites;
when Rapunzel pines and the prince comes forth,
or the Snow Queen sighs in the bitter north;
when Rose Red snuggles against the bear,
and I lean against Mother and feel her hair.

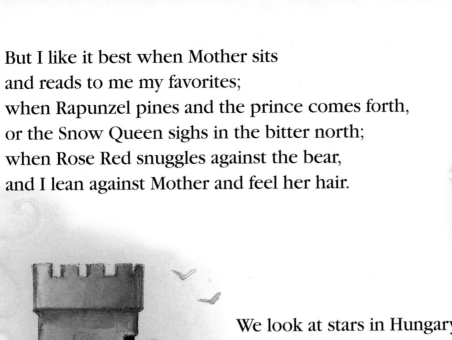

We look at stars in Hungary—
back of the North Wind—
over the sea—
the Nutcracker laughs;
the Erl King calls;
a wish comes true;
the beanstalk falls;
the Western wind blows sweet and low,
and Mother gives words to worlds I know.

Oral History

T. Marie Kryst   •   *illustrated by Gershom Griffith*

The first people to keep records and write down
the history and stories of their ancestors were
probably the ancient Egyptians and the
Chinese. But what about before that, before people
even knew how to write? How did people keep family
information?

Members of a clan or tribe gathered around
campfires and recited poetry and sang songs. Many of
these songs and poems told about family history.
Important names, brave deeds, and memorable events
were passed on to younger members of the group,
who remembered and memorized them for
safekeeping. This is called oral history because it is
history that is passed on by word of mouth instead of
being written down. It was the only way of keeping
family records before there was writing.

However, oral history thrives even today. The stories we hear from parents and grandparents as they remember the past are good examples of oral history in action. In certain areas of the world——Africa and some Pacific islands, for instance——oral history survives in a much more formal way. Many tribes or groups in West Africa have a griot, or village member who can recite the history of all the families in the village. If he should die, another has been trained to take his place so that history is not lost.

One report tells of a New Zealand tribal chief who had to recite the story of his people——thirty-four generations worth——in order to prove his right to land he had inherited. Some say his retelling took three days!

Another account tells of the longest oral history ever recited, covering seventy generations. This retelling was by an old man on an Indonesian island.

Island people are the most likely to have spoken records that go back such a long way. On an island, families were not as likely to move very far away, making it easier to keep track of family history.

However, if history, including family stories, is not remembered and retold, it will die out. In 1966, a group of high school students in Rabun Gap, Georgia, began a project that has become a well-known and much copied example of recording oral history. These students collected stories, songs, and mountain folklore from neighbors, family members, and other people who lived in their part of the Appalachian Mountains. They recorded traditional crafts and skills, such as banjo making and bear hunting. These spoken memories were published as a magazine called *Foxfire*. As the project continued every year, the magazine grew and became a series of Foxfire books. With these books, the students saved the rich history of an important piece of American life that might otherwise have been lost.

You can save your family's history, too. It's important to record what older members of the family remember so that your family's story won't be lost and forgotten. Here's how to begin:

1. First, make a list of three or four of the oldest living members of your family—great-grandparents or great-aunts and uncles would be wonderful. These might be people you've never met or don't know very well. Your parents can probably help.

2. Next, make a phone call or write a short note asking if they would be willing to talk with you about what they remember about their ancestors. If they live far away, you might ask them to write down any memories or information they think would be useful and send it to you by mail.

3. Find out from them if they know any other family members who might be helpful to you.

4. Make a list of questions that you want to have answered. This is a good way to spark their memories. But also let them just talk and tell stories about the past. They will enjoy it, and you will get some interesting information.

5. Record what these family members say. A tape recorder is usually the best way to do this, but you can also take notes. Get as many details as you can, such as first and middle names, parents' names, place names, and exact dates. This will help if you search for written records later.

You will still have a lot of work to do if you decide to continue your search. But this use of oral history will get you started on the road to piecing together the story of your family.

Oral History

Meet the Author

T. Marie Kryst is a former teacher who is now an editor and writer. She loves writing nonfiction articles and stories for children. When not working or writing, Kryst enjoys reading and playing the flute in a local community band. She and her husband, also an editor and writer, like to travel and go cross-country skiing. They have two grown children and reside in Skokie, Illinois, a suburb of Chicago.

Meet the Illustrator

Gershom Griffith was born in Barbados and moved to New York City when he was eleven. While there, he attended the High School of Art and Design, then went on to Mercy College. He says, *"From about the age of seven or eight, I knew I wanted to be an artist. In my teens, I realized I wanted to be an illustrator."* Gershom has had hundreds of his pictures published, and he has illustrated over 40 books. He currently lives in Florida with his wife and son.

Theme Connections

Within the Selection

Record your answers to the questions below in the Response Journal section of your Writer's Notebook. In small groups, report the ideas you wrote. Discuss your ideas with the rest of the group. Then choose a person to report your group's answers to the class.

- How does an oral history tell a story?
- How can you learn your family's oral history?

Across Selections

- How are Ananse's stories in "A Story A Story" like oral history? How are they different?

Beyond the Selection

- Do you think it is important to know the history of your family? What kinds of stories do you like to hear best? Who tells the most stories in your family?
- Think about how "Oral History" adds to what you know about storytelling.
- Add items to the Concept/Question Board about storytelling.

Storm in the Night

Mary Stolz
illustrated by Pat Cummings

Storm in the night.

Thunder like mountains blowing up.

Lightning licking the navy-blue sky.

Rain streaming down the windows, babbling in the downspouts.

And Grandfather?…And Thomas?…And Ringo, the cat?

They were in the dark.

Except for Ringo's shining mandarin eyes and the carrot-colored flames in the wood stove, they were quite in the dark.

"We can't read," said Grandfather.

"We can't look at TV," said Thomas.

"Too early to go to bed," said Grandfather.

Thomas sighed. "What will we do?"

"No help for it," said Grandfather, "I shall have to tell you a tale of when I was a boy."

Thomas smiled in the shadows.

It was not easy to believe that Grandfather had once been a boy, but Thomas believed it.

Because Grandfather said so, Thomas believed that long, long ago, probably at the beginning of the world, his grandfather had been a boy.

As Thomas was a boy now, and always would be.

A grandfather could be a boy, if he went back in his memory far enough; but a boy could not be a grandfather.

Ringo could not grow up to be a kangaroo, and a boy could not grow up to be an old man.

And that, said Thomas to himself, is that.

Grandfather was big and bearded.

Thomas had a chin as smooth as a peach.

Grandfather had a voice like a tuba.

Thomas's voice was like a penny whistle.

"I'm thinking," said Thomas.

"Ah," said Grandfather.

"I'm trying to think what you were like when you were my age."

"That's what I was like," said Grandfather.

"What?"

"Like someone your age."

"Did you look like me?"

"Very much like you."

"But you didn't have a beard."

"Not a sign of one."

"You were short, probably."

"Short, certainly."

"And your voice. It was like mine?"

"Exactly."

Thomas sighed. He just could not imagine it. He stopped trying.

He tried instead to decide whether to ask for a new story or an old one.

Grandfather knew more stories than a book full of stories.

Thomas hadn't heard all of them yet, because he kept asking for repeats.

As he thought about what to ask for, he listened to the sounds of the dark.

Grandfather listened too.

In the house a door creaked. A faucet leaked.

Ringo scratched on his post, then on Grandfather's chair.

He scratched behind his ear, and they could hear even that.

In the stove the flames made a fluttering noise.

"That's funny," said Thomas. "I can hear better in the dark than I can when the lights are on."

"No doubt because you are just listening," said his grandfather, "and not trying to see and hear at the same time."

That made sense to Thomas, and he went on listening for sounds in the dark.

There were the clocks.

The chiming clock on the mantel struck the hour of eight.

Ping, ping, ping, ping, ping, ping, ping, ping-a-ling.

The kitchen clock, very excited.

Tickticktickticktickticketу.

There were outside sounds for the listening, too.

The bells in the Congregational church rang through the rain.

Bong, bong, bong, bong, bong, bong, bong, BONG!

Automobile tires swished on the rain-wet streets.

Horns honked and hollered.

A siren whined in the distance.

"Grandfather," said Thomas, "were there automobiles when you were a boy?"

"Were there *automobiles*!" Grandfather shouted. "How old do you think I am?"

"Well..." said Thomas.

"Next thing, you'll be asking if there was electricity when I was your age."

"Oh, Grandfather!" said Thomas, laughing.

After a while he said, "Was there?"

"Let's go out on the porch," said Grandfather. "There's too much silliness in here."

By the light of the lightning they made their way to the front door and out on the porch.

Ringo, who always followed Thomas, followed him and jumped to the railing.

The rain, driving hard against the back of the house, was scarcely sprinkling here.

But it whooped windily through the great beech tree on the lawn, brandishing branches, tearing off twigs.

It drenched the bushes, splashed in the birdbath, clattered on the tin roof like a million tacks.

Grandfather and Thomas sat on the swing, creaking back and forth, back and forth, as thunder boomed and lightning stabbed across the sky.

Ringo's fur rose, and he turned his head from side to side, his eyes wide and wild in the flashes that lit up the night.

The air smelled peppery and gardeny and new.

"That's funny," said Thomas. "I can smell better in the dark, too."

Thomas thought Grandfather answered, but he couldn't hear, as just then a bolt of lightning cracked into the big beech tree. It ripped off a mighty bough, which crashed to the ground.

This was too much for Ringo. He leaped onto Thomas's lap and shivered there.

"Poor boy," said Thomas. "He's frightened."

"I had a dog when I was a boy," said Grandfather. "He was so scared of storms that I had to hide under the bed with him when one came. He was afraid even to be frightened alone."

"*I'm* not afraid of *anything*," Thomas said, holding his cat close.

"Not many people can say that," said Grandfather. Then he added, "Well, I suppose anybody could *say* it."

"I'm not afraid of thunderstorms, like Ringo and your dog. What was his name?"

"Melvin."

"That's not a good name for a dog," Thomas said.

"I thought it was," Grandfather said calmly. "He was my dog."

"I like cats," said Thomas. "I want to own a *tiger*!"

"Not while you're living with me," said Grandfather.

"Okay," Thomas said. "Is there a story about Melvin?"

"There is. One very good one."

"Tell it," Thomas commanded. "Please, I mean."

"Well," said Grandfather, "when Melvin and I were pups together, I was just as afraid of storms as he was."

"No!" said Thomas.

"Yes," said Grandfather. "We can't all be brave as tigers."

"I guess not," Thomas agreed.

"So there we were, the two of us, hiding under beds whenever a storm came."

"Think of that..." said Thomas.

"That's what I'm doing," said Grandfather.

"Anyway, the day came when Melvin was out on some errand of his own, and I was doing my homework, when all at once, with only a rumble of warning...

down came the rain, *down* came the lightning, and all around and everywhere came the thunder."

"Wow," said Thomas. "What did you do?"

"Dove under the bed."

"But what about Melvin?"

"I'm *coming* to that," said Grandfather. "What-about-Melvin is what the story is *about*."

"I see," said Thomas. "This is pretty exciting."

"Well—it was then. Are you going to listen, or keep interrupting?"

"I think I'll listen," said Thomas.

"Good. Where was I?"

"Under the bed."

"So I was. Well, I lay there shivering at every clap of thunder, and I'm ashamed to say that it was some time before I even remembered that my poor little dog was all by himself out in the storm."

Thomas shook his head in the dark.

"And when I did remember," Grandfather went on, "I had the most awful time making myself wriggle out from under the bed and go looking for my father or my mother—to ask them to go out and find Melvin for me."

"Grandfather!"

"I told you I was afraid. This is a true story you're hearing, so I have to tell the truth."

"Of course," said Thomas, admiring his grandfather for telling a truth like *that*. "Did you find them?"

"I did not. They had gone out someplace for an hour or so, but I'd forgotten. Thomas, fear does strange things to people...makes them forget everything but how afraid they are. You wouldn't know about that, of course."

Thomas stroked his cat and said nothing.

"In any case," Grandfather went on, "there I was, alone and afraid in the kitchen, and there was my poor little dog alone and afraid in the storm."

"What did you *do*?" Thomas demanded.

"You didn't *leave* him out there, did you, Grandfather?"

"Thomas—I put on my raincoat and opened the kitchen door and stepped out on the back porch just as a flash of lightning shook the whole sky and a clap of thunder barreled down and a huge man *appeared* out of the darkness, holding Melvin in his arms!"

"Whew!"

"That man was seven feet tall and had a face like a crack in the ice."

"Grandfather! You said you were telling me a true story."

"It's true, because that's how he looked to me. He stood there, scowling at me, and said, 'Son, is this your dog?' and I nodded, because I was too scared to speak. 'If you don't take better care of him, you shouldn't have him at all,' said the terrible man. He pushed Melvin at me and stormed off into the dark."

"Gee," said Thomas. "That wasn't very fair. He didn't know you were frightened too. I mean, Grandfather, how old were you?"

"Just about your age."

"Well, some people my age can get pretty frightened."

"Not you, of course."

Thomas said nothing.

"Later on," Grandfather continued, "I realized that man wasn't seven feet tall, or even terrible. He was worried about the puppy, so he didn't stop to think about me."

"Well, I think he should have."

"People don't always do what they should, Thomas."

"What's the end of the story?"

"Oh, just what you'd imagine," Grandfather said carelessly. "Having overcome my fear enough to forget myself and think about Melvin, I wasn't afraid of storms anymore."

"Oh, good," said Thomas.

For a while they were silent.

The storm was spent. There were only flickers of lightning, mutterings of thunder, and a little patter of rain.

"When are the lights going to come on?" Thomas asked.

"You know as much as I do," said Grandfather.

"Maybe they won't come on for hours," said Thomas. "Maybe they won't come on until *tomorrow*!"

"Maybe not."

"Maybe they'll *never* come on again, and what will we do then?"

"We'll think of something," said Grandfather.

"Grandfather?"

"Yes, Thomas?"

"What I think...I think that maybe if you hadn't been here, and Ringo hadn't been here, and I was all alone in the house and there was a storm and the lights went out and didn't come on again for a long time, like this...I think maybe *then* I would be a *little* bit afraid."

"Perfectly natural," said Grandfather.

Thomas sighed.

Grandfather yawned.

Ringo jumped to the porch floor and walked daintily into the garden, shaking his legs.

After a while the lights came on.

They turned them off and went to bed.

Storm in the Night

Meet the Author

Mary Stolz was born in Boston but currently lives on the Gulf of Mexico, where there is nothing between her house and the ocean but *"pale sand and sea oats,"* she says. Her Uncle Bill, affectionately called "Unk," inspired her love for reading by buying her books until the age of 18. Stolz has written books for children and young adults for more than 60 years. Her first book was written while she was confined to her house due to an illness as a young woman. She believes that she will keep writing books as long as children still turn to books for answers.

Meet the Illustrator

Pat Cummings has illustrated and written children's books that represent a variety of cultural perspectives. She and her family were constantly moving from state to state and country to country, wherever her father's job with the army took them. While living in Germany, Cummings developed an interest in fantasy and fairy tales while she climbed the stairs of castles. She began drawing ballerinas in Germany and selling them to her friends for a nickel. It was then that she realized she could make a living doing what she enjoyed.

Theme Connections

Within the Selection

Record your answers to the questions below in the Response Journal section of your Writer's Notebook. In small groups, report the ideas you wrote. Discuss your ideas with the rest of the group. Then choose a person to report your group's answers to the class.

- Why was the stormy night a good night for storytelling?
- Thomas's grandfather knew many stories. Why do you think he chose to tell the one that he did?

Across Selections

- How did "Storm in the Night" remind you of what you learned in "Oral History"?

Beyond the Selection

- Have you ever heard a story about an older family member who had an experience similar to one that you have had? How did it make you feel?
- Think about how "Storm in the Night" adds to what you know about storytelling.
- Add items to the Concept/Question Board about storytelling.

Past

Arnold Adoff
illustrated by John Kanzler

I have all these parts stuffed in
me
like mama's chicken
and
biscuits,
and
daddy's apple pie, and a tasty
story
from the family
tree.
But I know that tomorrow
morning
I'll wake up
empty, and hungry for that
next
bite
of my new
day.

Carving the Pole

from *Totem Pole*
by Diane Hoyt-Goldsmith
photographs by Lawrence Migdale

David, in the woods near his home, wears a Tsimshian robe and headdress. The headdress has a frontlet carved in the shape of an eagle and is decorated with ermine skins.

My name is David. I live in a small town called Kingston in Washington State. In the summer, I like to hunt for salmonberries and blackberries in the fields near our house.

My father is an artist, a wood-carver. Ever since I was little, I have watched him take a piece of wood and carve a creature from it. Sometimes it is a wolf, sometimes a bear, and sometimes an eagle. The eagle is the symbol and totem of the Eagle Clan, which is our family group within our tribe.

My father is carving a totem pole for the Klallam Indians who live on the Port Gamble Reservation near our home. Although my father belongs to a different tribe, the Tsimshian, he was asked to carve the pole because of his skill. It is common among the Northwest Coast Indians for one tribe to invite an artist from another tribe to carve a pole for them. The pole will be made from a single log, forty feet long. It will have animals and figures carved on it, important characters from Klallam myths and legends.

146

My father says that a totem pole is like a signboard. He tells me that it is a system for passing on legends and stories from one generation to another for people who have no written language. A totem pole is like a library for a tribe!

The first step in making a totem pole is to find a straight tree. It must be wide enough to make a strong pole. The best trees for a totem pole have few branches. Where a branch joins the trunk a knot forms, making the carving very difficult.

Nearly all totem poles are carved from cedar logs. Cedar trees grow very straight and are common in the evergreen forests along the coastline near our home. The wood of the cedar is soft and easy to carve. It does not rot and insects will not destroy it. A totem pole carved from a cedar log can last a hundred years or more.

David and his father look for a tall, straight tree in the woods near their home.

After the right tree is found and cut down, all the branches are removed with an axe and the bark is stripped from the outside of the log. In the old days, the Indians had no saws or axes, so even cutting the tree down was a harder job than it is today. Back then, the carvers used a hammer and chisel to cut a wedge at the base of the tree. This weakened the tree, and in a strong wind storm, the tree would fall.

When the log is ready to be carved, my father makes a drawing of how the pole will look when it is finished. He draws the animals for the totem pole on a sheet of paper. He might begin by drawing each animal separately, but before he starts to carve he will draw a picture of how the completed pole will look.

Next he uses a stick of charcoal to make a drawing on the log itself. Then he stands up on the log to see how the figures and animals look. When he is satisfied with the drawing, he takes up his tools and begins to carve.

David's father carves a totem pole on the Klallam Reservation. He works from a drawing which he transfers onto the log. The charcoal outline of the Bear's eyebrows is visible on the wood.

The totem pole for the Klallam tribe has six figures, one on top of the other. At the very top of the pole is the Thunderbird. He brings good luck to the Klallam village. The Klallam people believe the Thunderbird lives on the Olympic mountain range, across the water from their reservation, in the place where the mountains touch the sky. They say that when Thunderbird catches the great Killer Whale, you can hear thunder and see lightning in the sky.

Below Thunderbird is the figure who represents the Klallam people. The figure holds Killer Whale by the tail. Together, they tell the legend of a tribal member named Charlie who rode out to sea on the back of a Killer Whale.

The fourth animal on the pole is Bear, who provided the Indian people with many important things. His fur gave warmth and clothing. His meat gave food. His claws and teeth were used for trinkets and charms and to decorate clothing.

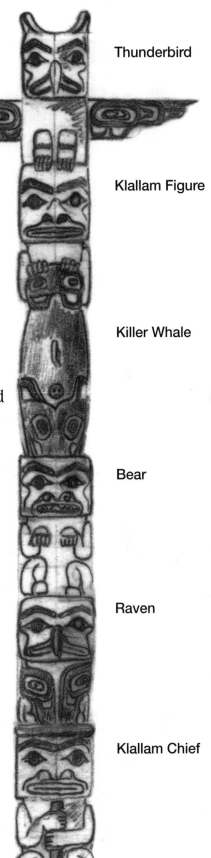

Thunderbird

Klallam Figure

Killer Whale

Bear

Raven

Klallam Chief

David and his father walk along the pole to check the progress of the carving. Kneeling on top, David learns to judge whether the figures on the pole are lined up correctly.

The next figure is Raven, who brought light to the Indian people by stealing the Sun from Darkness. Raven is the great trickster. Sometimes he does things that are good, but sometimes he does things that are bad.

The last figure on the pole is a Klallam Chief. The chief on the pole holds a "speaker stick," a symbol of his leadership and his important position in the tribe. In the Klallam culture, when a chief holds the speaker stick, all the people pay attention and listen to what he says.

As my father carves the pole, he brings all of these characters to life. He works on the pole every day. He uses many tools: the adze, chisels, and handmade knives. He even uses a chain saw for the largest cuts!

This totem pole is special to me. I am finally old enough to help my father with the work. He lets me sweep away the wood shavings as he carves. I can also take care of the tools he uses—the adze, the saws, the handmade knives, and the chisels.

As I get older, I'll learn how to use my father's carving tools safely and to help him really carve a pole. But for now, I just practice on some bits of wood I find lying around. Like my father, I look for the animal shapes hidden inside the wood.

Using a handmade knife, David's father carves fine details into the pole.

Striking the wood with the adze makes a unique pattern on the pole. This pattern differs with every carver and is like a signature of the artist who carves the pole.

In the old days, it used to take a year to carve a totem pole. In those days, the blade of the adze was made of stone and wasn't nearly as sharp as the steel blades my father uses today. Knives, for the carving of fine details, were made from beaver teeth or from large shells.

My father says that it is the artist's skill with the adze that makes a totem pole great. Each artist has his own way of carving. The strokes of the adze create a pattern in the wood, like small ripples across the wide water.

In the old days, carvers had special songs to chant while they worked. The chanting helped them keep up a rhythm with their adzing strokes. Now my father likes to work to songs on the radio. He works to the beat of rock 'n' roll.

My father makes the work look easy. He cuts into the wood quickly, as if it were as soft as soap. I know carving is much harder than he makes it look. I know because I've tried it.

This box was made by David's great-great-grandfather as a storage box for food. Now David's father uses it as a toolbox. The adzes in front are made from the elbows of alder or yew tree branches.

151

After all the figures and animals are carved into the log, I help my father paint the pole. We make the eyes dark. We paint the mouths red. Whale's back and dorsal fin are black. Raven and Thunderbird have wings with patterns of red and black. The colors my father shows me are taken from the old traditions of the Tsimshian people. From a distance, the pole will look powerful and strong.

Finally, after two months of hard work, my father puts away his tools and packs up his paintbrushes. The totem pole is finished.

David paints the eye shape of the Klallam Figure black.

The completed totem pole greets travelers who journey to the Klallam Reservation. The figures on the pole are Thunderbird at the top, then a Klallam Figure holding Killer Whale by the tail, then Bear, Raven, and the Klallam Chief with his speaker stick.

Carving the Pole

Meet the Author

Diane Hoyt-Goldsmith was interested in books at a very young age. In college, she began learning about book design. After college, she started designing books, and soon she was writing, too. *"The research for my books gives me the opportunity to travel to new places and develop new friendships. . . I love writing nonfiction because I enjoy learning about the world we live in. I like to meet new people and learn about their lives."*

Meet the Illustrator

Lawrence Migdale is a photographer. He says that he began taking photographs because *"the camera seemed to be the ideal excuse to meet and get to know the. . .different people I was encountering. It still is."* He likes to photograph people in a relaxed setting. Children looking at the pictures he takes have a better idea of what kind of life the characters in the story really have.

Theme Connections

Within the Selection

Record your answers to the questions below in the Response Journal section of your Writer's Notebook. In small groups, report the ideas you wrote. Discuss your ideas with the rest of the group. Then choose a person to report your group's answers to the class.

- How does a totem pole tell a story?
- David's father is an artist. How is he also a storyteller?

Across Selections

- How is "Carving the Pole" different from the other stories you have read about storytelling?
- Could you use your family's oral history to create a totem pole? What would it look like?

Beyond the Selection

- Think about how "Carving the Pole" adds to what you know about storytelling.
- Add items to the Concept/Question Board about storytelling.

Storyteller Doll. 1964. **Helen Cordero.** Slipped and painted earthenware. $8\frac{1}{4}$" high. The Museum of International Folk Art, Santa Fe, NM.

Anasazi culture petroglyphs, Petrified National Park, Arizona. **Anasazi Culture.** Photo: ©George H. H. Huey.

The Bearer of a Flag of Truce and the Medjeles, or the Council of Arab Chiefs. 1834. **Horace Vernet.** Oil on canvas. Musée Condé, Chantilly, France.

Bayeux Tapestry. Detail of Norman Cavalry Charging in the Battle of Hastings. 1070–1080. Embroidered wool on linen. Musée de la Reine Mathilde, Bayeux, France.

Focus Questions What item from your family represents
something of your family's past or of your family's traditions?
How do you think your family has changed over the years?
How do family stories help you remember the changes?

The Keeping Quilt

by Patricia Polacco

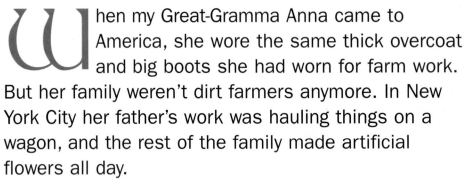

hen my Great-Gramma Anna came to
America, she wore the same thick overcoat
and big boots she had worn for farm work.
But her family weren't dirt farmers anymore. In New
York City her father's work was hauling things on a
wagon, and the rest of the family made artificial
flowers all day.

Everyone was in a hurry, and it was so crowded,
not like in backhome Russia. But all the same it was
their home, and most of their neighbors were just
like them.

When Anna went to school, English
sounded to her like pebbles dropping into
shallow water. *Shhhhhh. . . .*
·Shhhhhh. . . . Shhhhhh.
In six months
she was speaking
English.
Her parents almost
never learned, so she
spoke English for them, too.

The only things she had left of backhome Russia were her dress and the babushka she liked to throw up into the air when she was dancing.

And her dress was getting too small. After her mother had sewn her a new one, she took her old dress and babushka. Then from a basket of old clothes she took Uncle Vladimir's shirt, Aunt Havalah's nightdress, and an apron of Aunt Natasha's.

"We will make a quilt to help us always remember home," Anna's mother said. "It will be like having the family in backhome Russia dance around us at night."

And so it was. Anna's mother invited all the neighborhood ladies. They cut out animals and flowers from the scraps of clothing. Anna kept the needles threaded and handed them to the ladies as they needed them. The border of the quilt was made of Anna's babushka.

On Friday nights Anna's mother would say the prayers that started the Sabbath. The family ate challah and chicken soup. The quilt was the tablecloth.

Anna grew up and fell in love with Great-Grandpa Sasha. To show he wanted to be her husband, he gave Anna a gold coin, a dried flower, and a piece of rock salt, all tied into a linen handkerchief. The gold was for wealth, the flower for love, and the salt so their lives would have flavor.

She accepted the hankie. They were engaged.

Under the wedding huppa, Anna and Sasha promised each other love and understanding. After the wedding, the men and women celebrated separately.

When my Grandma Carle was born, Anna wrapped her daughter in the quilt to welcome her warmly into the world. Carle was given a gift of gold, flower, salt, and bread. Gold so she would never know poverty, a flower so she would always

know love, salt so her life would always have flavor, and bread so that she would never know hunger.

Carle learned to keep the Sabbath and to cook and clean and do washing.

"Married you'll be someday," Anna told Carle, and . . . again the quilt became a wedding huppa, this time for Carle's wedding to Grandpa George. Men and women celebrated together, but they still did not dance together. In Carle's wedding bouquet was a gold coin, bread, and salt.

Carle and George moved to a farm in Michigan and Great-Gramma Anna came to live with them. The quilt once again wrapped a new little girl, Mary Ellen.

Mary Ellen called Anna, Lady Gramma. She had grown very old and was sick a lot of the time. The quilt kept her legs warm.

On Anna's ninety-eighth birthday, the cake was a kulich, a rich cake with raisins and candied fruit in it.

When Great-Gramma Anna died, prayers were said to lift her soul to heaven. My mother Mary Ellen was now grown up.

When Mary Ellen left home, she took the quilt with her.

When she became a bride, the quilt became her huppa. For the first time, friends who were not Jews came to the wedding. My mother wore a suit, but in her bouquet were gold, bread, and salt.

 The quilt welcomed me, Patricia, into the world . . . and it was the tablecloth for my first birthday party.

At night I would trace my fingers around the edges of each animal on the quilt before I went to sleep. I told my mother stories about the animals on the quilt.

She told me whose sleeve had made the horse, whose apron had made the chicken, whose dress had made the flowers, and whose babushka went around the edge of the quilt.

The quilt was a pretend cape when I was in the bullring, or sometimes a tent in the steaming Amazon jungle.

At my wedding to Enzo-Mario, men and women danced together. In my bouquet were gold, bread, and salt—and a sprinkle of wine, so I would always know laughter.

Twenty years ago I held Traci Denise in the quilt for the first time. Someday she, too, will leave home and she will take the quilt with her.

The Keeping Quilt

Meet the Author and Illustrator

Patricia Polacco had fond feelings about her family, whom she describes as marvelous storytellers. She says, *"My fondest memories are of sitting around a stove or open fire, eating apples and popping corn while listening to the old ones tell glorious stories about the past. . . . With each retelling our stories gained a little more OOMPH!"*

"The Keeping Quilt" is a true story about Polacco's great-grandmother Anna and the quilt Anna's mother made from the family's old clothes so that Anna would always remember the old country.

164

Theme Connections

Within the Selection

Record your answers to the questions below in the Response Journal section of your Writer's Notebook. In small groups, report the ideas you wrote. Discuss your ideas with the rest of the group. Then choose a person to report your group's answers to the class.

- Why did Anna's mother want to make a quilt with old clothes?
- How was the family story passed down in "The Keeping Quilt"?

Across Selections

- What are the different ways that stories were handed down in the other selections in this unit?

Beyond the Selection

- Do you have a quilt or another special item at home that is meaningful to you? What story does it tell?
- Think about how "The Keeping Quilt" adds to what you know about storytelling.
- Add items to the Concept/Question Board about storytelling.

Focus Questions How do stories of long ago affect how you feel today? How can stories from the past change our future?

Aunt Sue's Stories

Langston Hughes
illustrated by Gavin Curtis

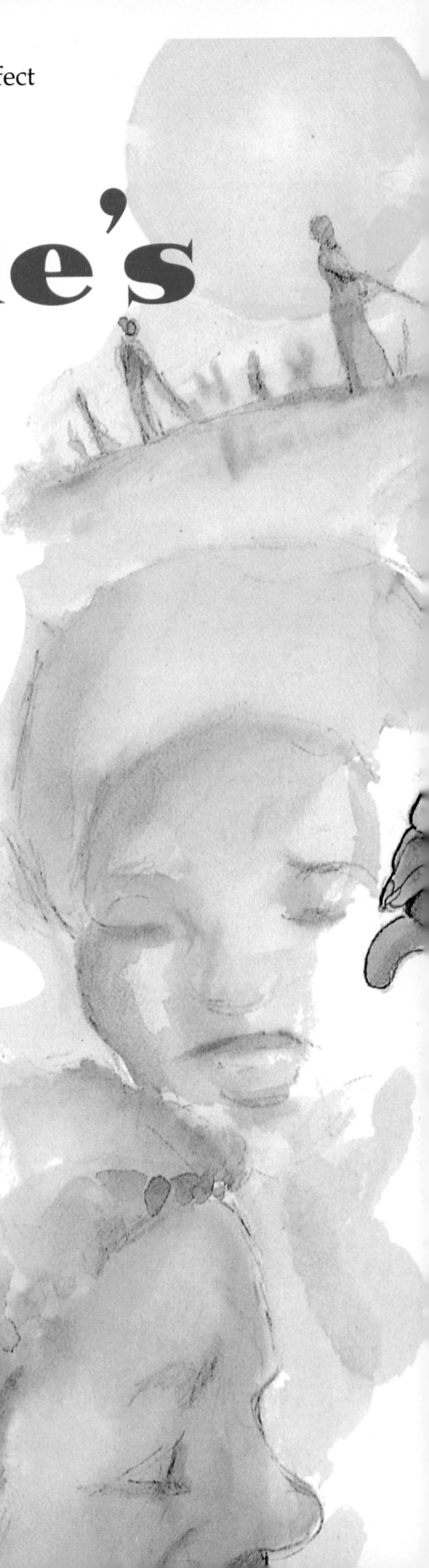

Aunt Sue has a head full of stories.
Aunt Sue has a whole heart full of stories.
Summer nights on the front porch
Aunt Sue cuddles a brown-faced child to her bosom
And tells him stories.

Black slaves
Working in the hot sun,
And black slaves
Walking in the dewy night,
And black slaves
Singing sorrow songs on the banks of a mighty river
Mingle themselves softly
In the flow of old Aunt Sue's voice,
Mingle themselves softly
In the dark shadows that cross and recross
Aunt Sue's stories.

And the dark-faced child, listening,
Knows that Aunt Sue's stories are real stories.
He knows that Aunt Sue
Never got her stories out of any book at all,
But that they came
Right out of her own life.

And the dark-faced child is quiet
Of a summer night
Listening to Aunt Sue's stories.

Focus Questions How important is it to tell a story exactly as it was told to you? Who are some men or women who have done great things and have had stories written about them? Why do some people become so well known that they have stories written about them?

JOHNNY APPLESEED

a tall tale retold and illustrated by Steven Kellogg

John Chapman, who later became known as Johnny Appleseed, was born on September 26, 1774, when the apples on the trees surrounding his home in Leominster, Massachusetts, were as red as the autumn leaves.

John's first years were hard. His father left the family to fight in the Revolutionary War, and his mother and his baby brother both died before his second birthday.

By the time John turned six, his father had remarried and settled in Longmeadow, Massachusetts. Within a decade their little house was overflowing with ten more children.

168

Nearby was an apple orchard. Like most early American families, the Chapmans picked their apples in the fall, stored them in the cellar for winter eating, and used them to make sauces, cider, vinegar, and apple butter. John loved to watch the spring blossoms slowly turn into the glowing fruit of autumn.

Watching the apples grow inspired in John a love of all of nature. He often escaped from his boisterous household to the tranquil woods. The animals sensed his gentleness and trusted him.

As soon as John was old enough to leave home, he set out to explore the vast wilderness to the west. When he reached the Allegheny Mountains, he cleared a plot of land and planted a small orchard with the pouch of apple seeds he had carried with him.

John walked hundreds of miles through the Pennsylvania forest, living like the Indians he befriended on the trail. As he traveled, he cleared the land for many more orchards. He was sure the pioneer families would be arriving before long, and he looked forward to supplying them with apple trees.

When a storm struck, he found shelter in a hollow log or built a lean-to. On clear nights he stretched out under the stars.

Over the next few years, John continued to visit and care for his new orchards. The winters slowed him down, but he survived happily on a diet of butternuts.

One spring he met a band of men who boasted that they could lick their weight in wildcats. They were amazed to hear that John wouldn't hurt an animal.

They challenged John to compete at wrestling, the favorite frontier sport. He suggested a more practical contest—a tree-chopping match. The woodsmen eagerly agreed.

When the sawdust settled, there was no question about who had come out on top.

John was pleased that the land for his largest orchard had been so quickly cleared. He thanked the exhausted woodsmen for their help and began planting.

During the next few years, John continued to move westward. Whenever he ran out of apple seeds, he hiked to the eastern cider presses to replenish his supply. Before long, John's plantings were spread across the state of Ohio.

Meanwhile, pioneer families were arriving in search of homesites and farmland. John had located his orchards on the routes he thought they'd be traveling. As he had hoped, the settlers were eager to buy his young trees.

John went out of his way to lend a helping hand to his new neighbors. Often he would give his trees away. People affectionately called him Johnny Appleseed, and he began using that name.

He particularly enjoyed entertaining children with tales of his wilderness adventures and stories.

In 1812 the British incited the Indians to join them in another war against the Americans. The settlers feared that Ohio would be invaded from Lake Erie.

It grieved Johnny that his friends were fighting each other. But when he saw the smoke of burning cabins, he ran through the night, shouting a warning at every door.

After the war, people urged Johnny to build a house and settle down. He replied that he lived like a king in his wilderness home, and he returned to the forest he loved.

During his long absences, folks enjoyed sharing their recollections of Johnny. They retold his stories and sometimes they even exaggerated them a bit.

Some recalled Johnny sleeping in a treetop hammock and chatting with the birds.

Others remembered that a rattlesnake had attacked his foot. Fortunately, Johnny's feet were as tough as elephant's hide, so the fangs didn't penetrate.

It was said that Johnny had once tended a wounded wolf and then kept him for a pet.

An old hunter swore he'd seen Johnny frolicking with a bear family.

The storytellers outdid each other with tall tales about his feats of survival in the untamed wilderness.

174

As the years passed, Ohio became too crowded for Johnny. He moved to the wilds of Indiana, where he continued to clear land for his orchards.

When the settlers began arriving, Johnny recognized some of the children who had listened to his stories. Now they had children of their own.

It made Johnny's old heart glad when they welcomed him as a beloved friend and asked to hear his tales again.

When Johnny passed seventy, it became difficult for him to keep up with his work. Then, in March of 1845, while trudging through a snowstorm near Fort Wayne, Indiana, he became ill for the first time in his life.

Johnny asked for shelter in a settler's cabin, and a few days later he died there.

Curiously, Johnny's stories continued to move westward without him. Folks maintained that they'd seen him in Illinois or that he'd greeted them in Missouri, Arkansas, or Texas. Others were certain that he'd planted trees on the slopes of the Rocky Mountains or in California's distant valleys.

Even today people still claim they've seen
Johnny Appleseed.

JOHNNY APPLESEED

Meet the Author and Illustrator

Steven Kellogg has been an animal lover for as long as he can remember. As a child, he always wanted a pet but wasn't allowed to have one. Now many of his books are about animals. His Pinkerton stories are about a real dog—a Great Dane. Steven got Pinkerton as a puppy and loved to watch his stubborn antics. Steven Kellogg wrote *Pinkerton Behave!* about his funny dog. Almost all the characters in Steven Kellogg's books are based on people or animals he knows.

Theme Connections

Within the Selection

Record your answers to the questions below in the Response Journal section of your Writer's Notebook. In small groups, report the ideas you wrote. Discuss your ideas with the rest of the group. Then choose a person to report your group's answers to the class.

- Many of the stories about Johnny Appleseed are legends about a real man named John Chapman. How did his life's story become a legend?
- How were Johnny's stories kept alive even after he had died?

Across Selections

- How is "Johnny Appleseed" like one of Ananse's stories?
- Compare the way history is retold in the stories of Johnny Appleseed and the way history is retold in an oral history.

Beyond the Selection

- Think about how "Johnny Appleseed" adds to what you know about storytelling.
- Add items to the Concept/Question Board about storytelling.

Aunt Flossie's Hats

(and Crab Cakes Later)

Elizabeth Fitzgerald Howard

illustrated by James Ransome

On Sunday afternoons, Sarah and I go to see Great-great-aunt Flossie. Sarah and I love Aunt Flossie's house. It is crowded full of stuff and things. Books and pictures and lamps and pillows . . . Plates and trays and old dried flowers . . . And boxes and boxes and boxes of HATS!

On Sunday afternoons when Sarah and I go to see Aunt Flossie, she says, "Come in, Susan. Come in, Sarah. Have some tea. Have some cookies. Later we can get some crab cakes!"

We sip our tea and eat our cookies, and then Aunt Flossie lets us look in her hatboxes.

We pick out hats and try them on. Aunt Flossie says they are her memories, and each hat has its story.

180

Hats, hats, hats, hats! A stiff black one with bright red ribbons. A soft brown one with silver buttons. Thin floppy hats that hide our eyes. Green or blue or pink or purple. Some have fur and some have feathers. Look! This hat is just one smooth soft rose, but here's one with a trillion flowers! Aunt Flossie has so many hats!

One Sunday afternoon, I picked out a wooly winter hat, sort of green, maybe. Aunt Flossie thought a minute. Aunt Flossie almost always thinks a minute before she starts a hat story. Then she sniffed the wooly hat. "Just a little smoky smell now," she said.

Sarah and I sniffed the hat, too. "Smoky smell, Aunt Flossie?"

"The big fire," Aunt Flossie said. "The big fire in Baltimore. Everything smelled of smoke for miles around. For days and days. Big fire. Didn't come near our house on Centre Street, but we could hear fire engines racing down St. Paul. Horses' hooves clattering. Bells! Whistles! Your great-grandma and I couldn't sleep. We grabbed our coats and hats and

182

ran outside. Worried about Uncle Jimmy's grocery store, worried about the terrapins and crabs. Big fire in Baltimore."

Aunt Flossie closed her eyes. I think she was seeing long ago. I wondered about crab cakes. Did they have crab cakes way back then? Then Sarah sniffed Aunt Flossie's hat. "No more smoky smell," she said. But I thought I could smell some, just a little.

Then Sarah tried a different hat. Dark, dark blue, with a red feather. "This one, Aunt Flossie! This one!"

Aunt Flossie closed her eyes and thought a minute. "Oh my, yes, my, my. What an exciting day!"

We waited, Sarah and I. "What happened, Aunt Flossie?" I asked.

"Big parade in Baltimore."

"Ooh! Parade!" said Sarah. "We love parades."

"I made that hat," Aunt Flossie said, "to wear to watch that big parade. Buglers bugling. Drummers drumming. Flags flying everywhere. The boys—soldiers, you know—back from France. Marching up Charles Street. Proud. Everyone cheering, everyone shouting! The Great War was over! The Great War was over!"

"Let's have a parade!" I said. Sarah put on the dark blue hat. I found a red one with a furry pompom. We marched around Aunt Flossie's house.

"March with us, Aunt Flossie!" I called. But she was closing her eyes. She was seeing long ago. "Maybe she's dreaming about crab cakes," Sarah said.

Then we looked in the very special box. "Look, Aunt Flossie! Here's your special hat." It was the big straw hat with the pink and yellow flowers and green velvet ribbon. Aunt Flossie's favorite best Sunday hat! It's our favorite story, because we are in the story, and we can help Aunt Flossie tell it!

Aunt Flossie smiled. "One Sunday afternoon," she said, "we were going out for crab cakes. Sarah and Susan . . ."

"And Mommy and Daddy," I said.

"And Aunt Flossie," said Sarah.

Aunt Flossie nodded. "We were walking by the water. And the wind came."

"Let me tell it," I said. "The wind came and blew away your favorite best Sunday hat!"

"My favorite best Sunday hat," said Aunt Flossie. "It landed in the water."

"It was funny," said Sarah.

"I didn't think so," said Aunt Flossie.

"And Daddy tried to reach it," I said, "but he slid down in the mud. Daddy looked really surprised, and everybody laughed."

"He couldn't rescue my favorite, favorite best Sunday hat," said Aunt Flossie.

"And Mommy got a stick and leaned far out. She almost fell in, but she couldn't reach it either. The water rippled, and your favorite best Sunday hat just floated by like a boat!"

"Now comes the best part, and I'll tell it!" said Sarah. "A big brown dog came. It was walking with a boy. 'May we help you?' the boy asked. 'My dog Gretchen can get it.' The boy threw a small, small

stone. It landed in Aunt Flossie's hat! 'Fetch, Gretchen, fetch! Fetch, Gretchen, fetch!' Gretchen jumped into the water and she swam. She swam and she got it! Gretchen got Aunt Flossie's hat! 'Hurray for Gretchen!' We all jumped up and down. 'Hurray for Aunt Flossie's hat!' "

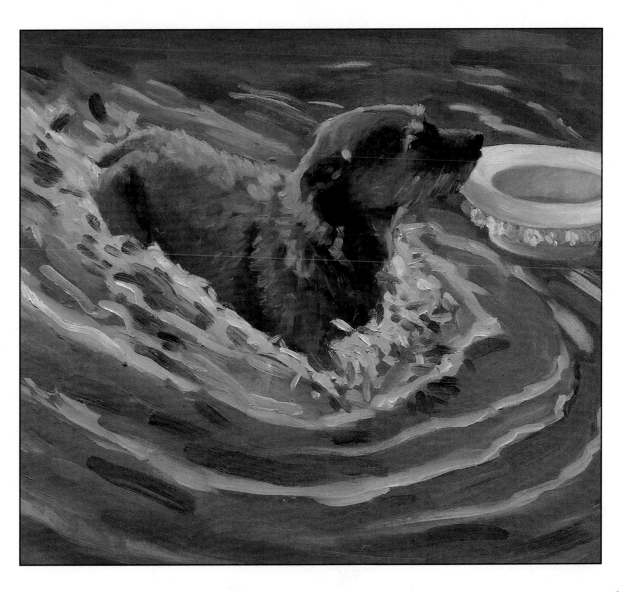

"It was very wet," said Aunt Flossie, "but it dried just fine . . . almost like new. My favorite, favorite best Sunday hat."

"I like that story," I said.

"So do I," said Sarah. "And I like what happened next! We went to get crab cakes!"

"Crab cakes!" said Aunt Flossie. "What a wonderful idea! Sarah, Susan, telephone your parents. We'll go get some crab cakes right now!"

I think Sarah and I will always agree about one thing: Nothing in the whole wide world tastes as good as crab cakes.

But crab cakes taste best after stories . . . stories about Aunt Flossie's hats!

Aunt Flossie's Hats
❦ (and Crab Cakes Later) ❧

Meet the Author

Elizabeth Fitzgerald Howard got the idea for "Aunt Flossie's Hats" from her fond memory of a family visit to the Inner Harbor in Baltimore. There the real Aunt Flossie lost her "favorite best Sunday hat" to the wind, resulting in a mad scramble to retrieve it. Howard's Aunt Flossie Wright was a Baltimore schoolteacher who *"lived in the same house most of her life," "knew everyone,"* and *"never threw anything away."* Howard says her Aunt Flossie always had stories to tell about the old days.

Meet the Illustrator

James Ransome enjoys illustrating books for children. *"I try to add things to the illustration that the writer couldn't put in the story. Aunt Flossie liked to collect things, so I tried to put a lot of old things in the house—paintings of old relatives, china, and other knickknacks."* Color is also important to Ransome. *"I tried to convey the warmth of home and family through a generous use of earth tones."*

Theme Connections

Within the Selection

Record your answers to the questions below in the Response Journal section of your Writer's Notebook. In small groups, report the ideas you wrote. Discuss your ideas with the rest of the group. Then choose a person to report your group's answers to the class.

- How can Aunt Flossie's hats be memories?
- How did Aunt Flossie's favorite hat turn Susan, Sarah, and Aunt Flossie into storytellers?

Across Selections

- What other stories have you read about storytelling?
- How is "Aunt Flossie's Hats" like "Carving the Pole"?

Beyond the Selection

- Can you think of an object that reminds you of an important event in your life? What story does it tell?
- Think about how "Aunt Flossie's Hats" adds to what you know about storytelling.
- Add items to the Concept/Question Board about storytelling.

Focus Questions What kind of stories might a very old tree have to tell? How can you listen to and learn from old trees?

Lemon Tree

Jennifer Clement
translated by Consuelo de Aerenlund
illustrated by Joanna Borrero

If you climb a lemon tree
feel the bark
under your knees and feet,
smell the white flowers,
rub the leaves
in your hands.
Remember,
the tree is older than you are
and you might find stories
in its branches.

194

Árbol de limón

Si te subes a un árbol de limón
siente la corteza
con tus rodillas y pies,
huele sus flores blancas,
talla las hojas
entre tus manos.
Recuerda,
el árbol es mayor que tú
y tal vez encuentres cuentos
entre sus ramas.

195

Some people live in the
city, and others live in the
country. Living in the country
long ago was different from
living in the country today.
What is the difference? Why
is it different?

The Country Mouse and the City Mouse

from *Aesop's Fables*
by Heidi Holder

An honest, plain, sensible Country Mouse invited her city friend for a visit. When the City Mouse arrived, the Country Mouse opened her heart and hearth in honor of her old friend. There was not a morsel that she did not bring forth out of her larder—peas and barley, cheese parings and nuts—hoping by quantity to make up for what she feared was wanting in quality, eating nothing herself, lest her guest should not have enough.

198

The City Mouse, condescending to pick a bit here and a bit there, at length exclaimed, "My dear, please let me speak freely to you. How can you endure the dullness of your life here, with nothing but woods and meadows, mountains and brooks about? You can't really prefer these empty fields to streets teeming with carriages and men! Do you not long for the conversation of the world instead of the chirping of birds? I promise you will find the city a change for the better. Let's away this moment!"

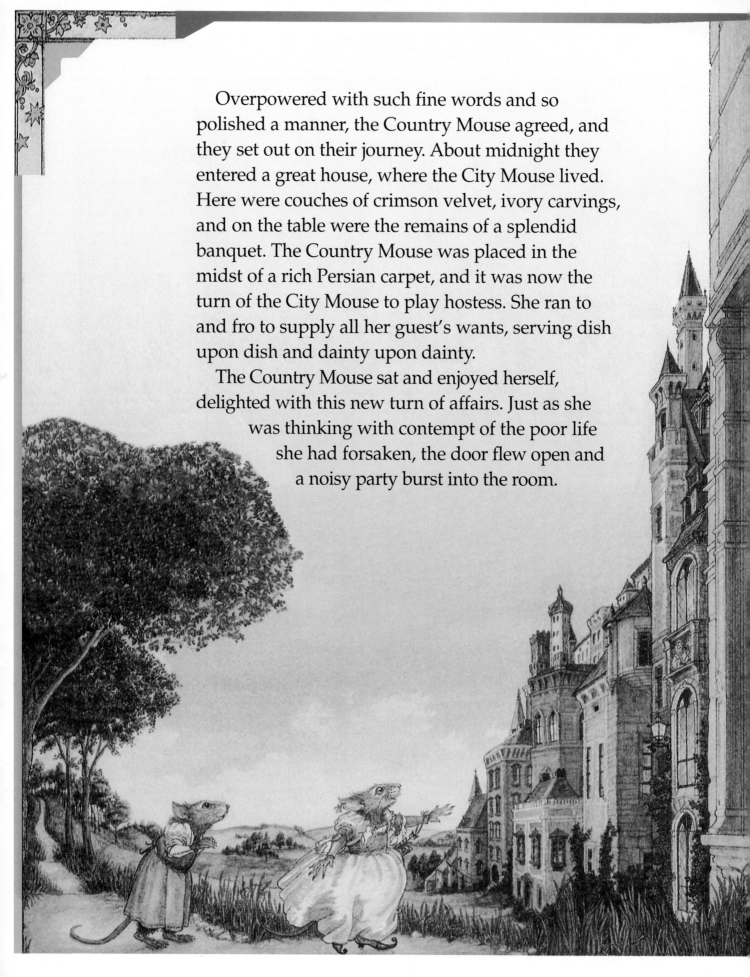

Overpowered with such fine words and so polished a manner, the Country Mouse agreed, and they set out on their journey. About midnight they entered a great house, where the City Mouse lived. Here were couches of crimson velvet, ivory carvings, and on the table were the remains of a splendid banquet. The Country Mouse was placed in the midst of a rich Persian carpet, and it was now the turn of the City Mouse to play hostess. She ran to and fro to supply all her guest's wants, serving dish upon dish and dainty upon dainty.

The Country Mouse sat and enjoyed herself, delighted with this new turn of affairs. Just as she was thinking with contempt of the poor life she had forsaken, the door flew open and a noisy party burst into the room.

The frightened friends scurried for the first corner they could find. No sooner did they peek out than the barking of dogs drove them back in greater terror than before. At length, when things seemed quiet, the Country Mouse stole from her hiding place and bade her friend good-bye, whispering, "Oh, my dear, this fine mode of living may do for you, but I prefer my poor barley in peace and quiet to dining at the richest feast where Fear and Danger lie waiting."

A simple life in peace and safety is preferable to a life of luxury tortured by fear.

The Country Mouse and the City Mouse

Meet the Author

Aesop lived between approximately 620 and 560 B.C. He was known for traveling throughout Asia Minor telling wise and entertaining animal fables. Many popular words and phrases come from Aesop's fables: "sour grapes," "proud as a peacock," and "don't count your chickens before they're hatched." Aesop's fables are known for teaching rules and moral lessons about life and human behavior.

Meet the Illustrator

Heidi Holder has always loved animals. She began drawing animals for her own pleasure. Illustrating selections of *Aesop's Fables* gave her the opportunity to show her talents at using color and drawing mood and setting. Heidi lives in New York City with her cats, dogs, birds, ducks, rabbits, and newts.

Theme Connections

Within the Selection

Record your answers to the questions below in the Response Journal section of your Writer's Notebook. In small groups, report the ideas you wrote. Discuss your ideas with the rest of the group. Then choose a person to report your group's answers to the class.

- Why did the Country Mouse want to go to the city?
- What made the Country Mouse want to go back to her country life?

Beyond the Selection

- Have you ever wanted to live somewhere else? Why?
- Think about how "The Country Mouse and the City Mouse" adds to what you know about country life.
- Add items to the Concept/Question Board about country life.

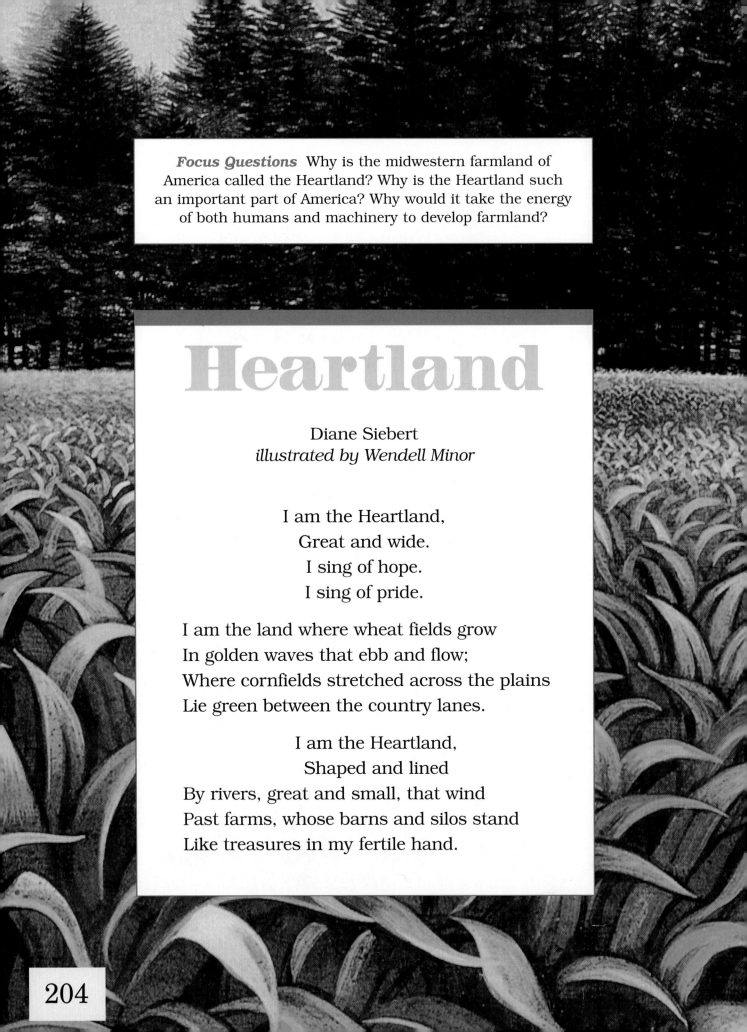

Heartland

Diane Siebert
illustrated by Wendell Minor

I am the Heartland,
Great and wide.
I sing of hope.
I sing of pride.

I am the land where wheat fields grow
In golden waves that ebb and flow;
Where cornfields stretched across the plains
Lie green between the country lanes.

I am the Heartland,
Shaped and lined
By rivers, great and small, that wind
Past farms, whose barns and silos stand
Like treasures in my fertile hand.

204

I am the Heartland.
I can feel
Machines of iron, tools of steel,
Creating farmlands, square by square—
A quilt of life I proudly wear:

A patchwork quilt laid gently down
In hues of yellow, green, and brown
As tractors, plows, and planters go
Across my fields and, row by row,
Prepare the earth and plant the seeds
That grow to meet a nation's needs.

A patchwork quilt whose seams are etched
By miles of wood and wire stretched
Around the barns and pastures where
The smell of livestock fills the air.
These are the farms where hogs are bred,
The farms where chicks are hatched and fed;
The farms where dairy cows are raised,
The farms where cattle herds are grazed;
The farms with horses, farms with sheep—
Upon myself, all these I keep.

I am the Heartland.
On this soil
Live those who through the seasons toil:

The farmer, with his spirit strong;
The farmer, working hard and long,
A feed-and-seed-store cap in place,
Pulled down to shield a weathered face—
A face whose every crease and line
Can tell a tale, and help define
A lifetime spent beneath the sun,
A life of work that's never done.

I am the Heartland.
On these plains
Rise elevators filled with grains.
They mark the towns where people walk
To see their neighbors, just to talk;
Where farmers go to get supplies
And sit a spell to analyze
The going price of corn and beans,
The rising cost of new machines;
Where steps are meant for shelling peas,
And kids build houses in the trees.

I am the Heartland.
In my song
Are cities beating, steady, strong,
With footsteps from a million feet
And sounds of traffic in the street;
Where giant mills and stockyards sprawl,
And neon-lighted shadows fall
From windowed walls of brick that rise
Toward the clouds, to scrape the skies;
Where highways meet and rails converge;
Where farm and city rhythms merge
To form a vital bond between
The concrete and the fields of green.

I am the Heartland:
Earth and sky
And changing seasons passing by.

I feel the touch of autumn's chill,
And as its colors brightly spill
Across the land, the growing ends,

And winter, white and cold, descends
With blizzards howling as they sweep
Across me, piling snowdrifts deep.
Then days grow longer, skies turn clear,
And all the gifts of spring appear——
The young are born, the seedlings sprout;

Before me, summer stretches out
With pastures draped in lush, green grass,
And as the days of growing pass,
I feel the joy when fields of grain
Are blessed by sunlight, warmth, and rain;

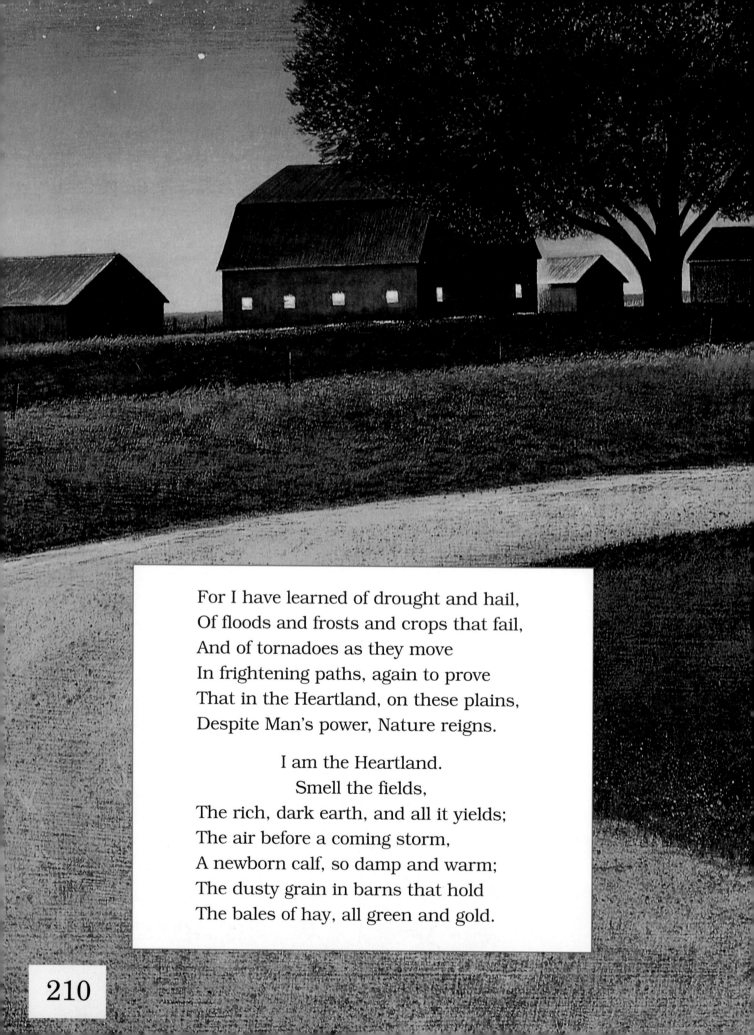

For I have learned of drought and hail,
Of floods and frosts and crops that fail,
And of tornadoes as they move
In frightening paths, again to prove
That in the Heartland, on these plains,
Despite Man's power, Nature reigns.

I am the Heartland.
Smell the fields,
The rich, dark earth, and all it yields;
The air before a coming storm,
A newborn calf, so damp and warm;
The dusty grain in barns that hold
The bales of hay, all green and gold.

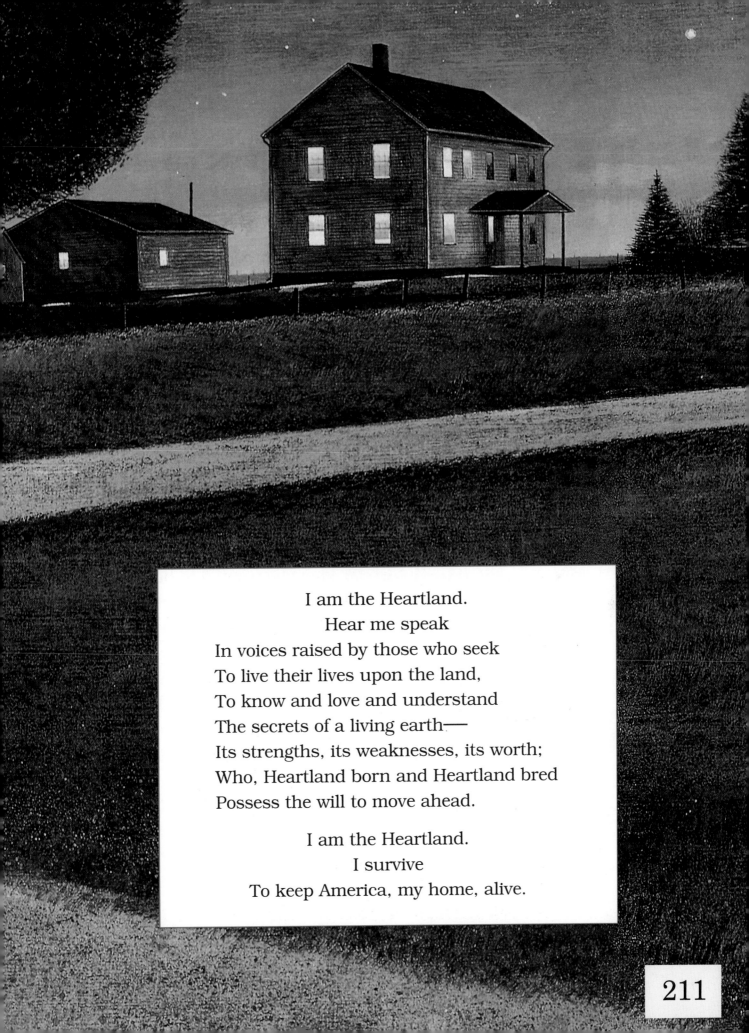

I am the Heartland.
Hear me speak
In voices raised by those who seek
To live their lives upon the land,
To know and love and understand
The secrets of a living earth—
Its strengths, its weaknesses, its worth;
Who, Heartland born and Heartland bred
Possess the will to move ahead.

I am the Heartland.
I survive
To keep America, my home, alive.

Heartland

Meet the Author

Diane Siebert's love of travel, people, the environment and music has provided her inspiration for her award-winning children's books. As she and her husband traveled throughout the United States and Mexico, she recorded her thoughts and feelings in a journal. Diane says: *"I wrote about what I was seeing and hearing and about all that was good and all that was bad. Some of it came out in prose, some in poetry, and some in song."* She and her husband live in Oregon with their six dogs and pet rats.

Meet the Illustrator

Wendell Minor knew he wanted to be an artist when he was nine years old. He studied art throughout school and graduated from the Ringling School of Art and Design. Since 1970, he has designed more than 1,000 book jackets. One of Wendell's primary interests is helping children learn more about the environment. Wendell has won more than 200 awards, has designed stamps for the U.S. Postal Service and was chosen by NASA to illustrate the space shuttle Discovery's return to flight.

Theme Connections

Within the Selection

Record your answers to the questions below in the Response Journal section of your Writer's Notebook. In small groups, report the ideas you wrote. Discuss your ideas with the rest of the group. Then choose a person to report your group's answers to the class.

- How does a patchwork quilt describe country life?
- Although people use farm machinery and build cities on the Heartland to make their lives easier, what is always a threat to a comfortable country life?

Across Selections

- How is "Heartland" different from the other selections you have read?

Beyond the Selection

- Think about what "Heartland" tells you about country life.
- Add items to the Concept/Question Board about country life.

Rudolph Is Tired of the City

Gwendolyn Brooks
illustrated by Anna Rich

These buildings are too close to me.
I'd like to PUSH away.
I'd like to live in the country,
And spread my arms all day.

I'd like to spread my breath out, too—
As farmers' sons and daughters do.

I'd tend the cows and chickens.
I'd do the other chores.
Then, all the hours left I'd go
A-SPREADING out-of-doors.

Focus Questions How would hard times affect the lives of those living and working on a farm? What would you do if you knew giving up something important to you would help your family or friends?

Leah's Pony

Elizabeth Friedrich

illustrated by Michael Garland

The year the corn grew tall and straight, Leah's papa bought her a pony. The pony was strong and swift and sturdy, with just a snip of white at the end of his soft black nose. Papa taught Leah to place her new saddle right in the middle of his back and tighten the girth around his belly, just so.

That whole summer, Leah and her pony crossed through cloud-capped cornfields and chased cattle through the pasture.

Leah scratched that special spot under her pony's mane and brushed him till his coat glistened like satin.

Each day Leah loved to ride her pony into town just to hear Mr. B. shout from the door of his grocery store, "That's the finest pony in the whole county."

The year the corn grew no taller than a man's thumb, Leah's house became very quiet. Sometimes on those hot, dry nights, Leah heard Papa and Mama's hushed voices whispering in the kitchen. She couldn't understand the words but knew their sad sound.

Some days the wind blew so hard it turned the sky black with dust. It was hard for Leah to keep her pony's coat shining. It was hard for Mama to keep the house clean. It was hard for Papa to carry buckets of water for the sow and her piglets.

Soon Papa sold the pigs and even some of the cattle. "These are hard times," he told Leah with a puzzled look. "That's what these days are, all right, hard times."

Mama used flour sacks to make underwear for Leah. Mama threw dishwater on her drooping petunias to keep them growing. And, no matter what else happened, Mama always woke Leah on Saturday with the smell of fresh, hot coffee cake baking.

One hot, dry, dusty day grasshoppers turned the day to night. They ate the trees bare and left only twigs behind.

The next day the neighbors filled their truck with all they owned and stopped to say good-bye. "We're off to Oregon," they said. "It must be better there." Papa, Mama, and Leah waved as their neighbors wobbled down the road in an old truck overflowing with chairs and bedsprings and wire.

The hot, dry, dusty days kept coming. On a day you could almost taste the earth in the air, Papa said, "I have something to tell you, Leah, and I want you to be brave. I borrowed money from the bank. I bought seeds, but the seeds dried up and blew away. Nothing grew. I don't have any corn to sell. Now I can't pay back the bank," Papa paused. "They're going to have an auction, Leah. They're going to sell the cattle and the chickens and the pickup truck."

Leah stared at Papa. His voice grew husky and soft. "Worst of all, they're going to sell my tractor. I'll never be able to plant corn when she's gone. Without my tractor, we might even have to leave the farm. I told you, Leah, these are hard times."

Leah knew what an auction meant. She knew eager faces with strange voices would come to their farm. They would stand outside and offer money for Papa's best bull and Mama's prize rooster and Leah's favorite calf.

All week Leah worried and waited and wondered what to do. One morning she watched as a man in a big hat hammered a sign into the ground in front of her house.

Leah wanted to run away. She raced her pony past empty fields lined with dry gullies. She galloped past a house with rags stuffed in broken windowpanes. She sped right past Mr. B. sweeping the steps outside his store.

At last Leah knew what she had to do. She turned her pony around and rode back into town. She stopped in front of Mr. B.'s store. "You can buy my pony," she said.

Mr. B. stopped sweeping and stared at her. "Why would you want to sell him?" he asked. "That's the finest pony in the county."

Leah swallowed hard. "I've grown a lot this summer," she said. "I'm getting too big for him."

Sunburned soil crunched under Leah's feet as she walked home alone. The auction had begun. Neighbors, friends, strangers—everyone clustered around the man in the big hat. "How much for this wagon?" boomed the man. "Five dollars. Ten dollars. Sold for fifteen dollars to the man in the green shirt."

Papa's best bull.

Sold.

Mama's prize rooster.

Sold.

Leah's favorite calf.

Sold.

Leah clutched her money in her hand. "It has to be enough," she whispered to herself. "It just has to be."

"Here's one of the best items in this entire auction," yelled the man in the big hat. "Who'll start the bidding at five hundred dollars for this practically new, all-purpose Farmall tractor? It'll plow, plant, fertilize, and even cultivate for you."

It was time. Leah's voice shook. "One dollar."

The man in the big hat laughed. "That's a low starting bid if I ever heard one," he said. "Now let's hear some serious bids."

No one moved. No one said a word. No one even seemed to breathe.

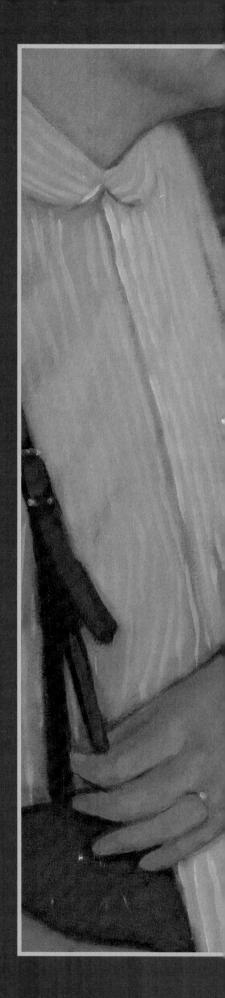

"Ladies and gentlemen, this tractor is a beauty! I have a bid of only one dollar for it. One dollar for this practically new Farmall tractor! Do I hear any other bids?"

Again no one moved. No one said a word. No one even seemed to breathe.

"This is ridiculous!" the man's voice boomed out from under his hat into the silence. "Sold to the young lady for one dollar."

The crowd cheered. Papa's mouth hung open. Mama cried. Leah proudly walked up and handed one dollar to the auctioneer in the big hat.

"That young lady bought one fine tractor for one very low price," the man continued. "Now how much am I bid for this flock of healthy young chickens?"

"I'll give you ten cents," offered a farmer who lived down the road.

"Ten cents! Ten cents is mighty cheap for a whole flock of chickens," the man said. His face looked angry.

Again no one moved. No one said a word. No one even seemed to breathe.

"Sold for ten cents!"

The farmer picked up the cage filled with chickens and walked over to Mama. "These chickens are yours," he said.

The man pushed his big hat back on his head. "How much for this good Ford pickup truck?" he asked.

"Twenty-five cents," yelled a neighbor from town.

Again no one moved. No one said a word. No one even seemed to breathe.

"Sold for twenty-five cents!" The man in the big hat shook his head. "This isn't supposed to be a penny auction!" he shouted.

The neighbor paid his twenty-five cents and took the keys to the pickup truck. "I think these will start your truck," he whispered as he dropped the keys into Papa's shirt pocket.

Leah watched as friends and neighbors bid a penny for a chicken or a nickel for a cow or a quarter for a plow. One by one, they gave everything back to Mama and Papa.

The crowds left. The sign disappeared. Chickens scratched in their coop, and cattle called for their corn. The farm was quiet. Too quiet. No familiar whinny greeted Leah when she entered the barn. Leah swallowed hard and straightened her back.

That night in Leah's hushed house, no sad voices whispered in the kitchen. Only Leah lay awake, listening to the clock chime nine and even ten times. Leah's heart seemed to copy its slow, sad beat.

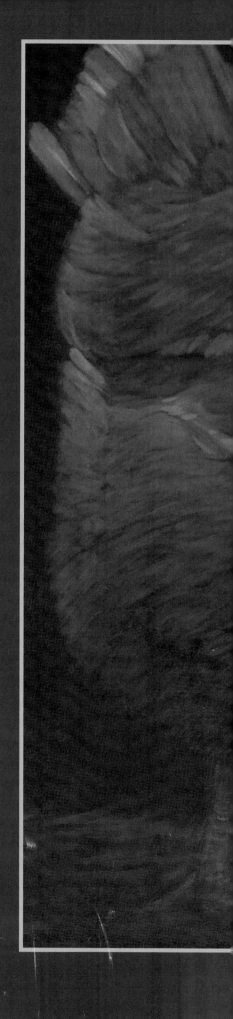

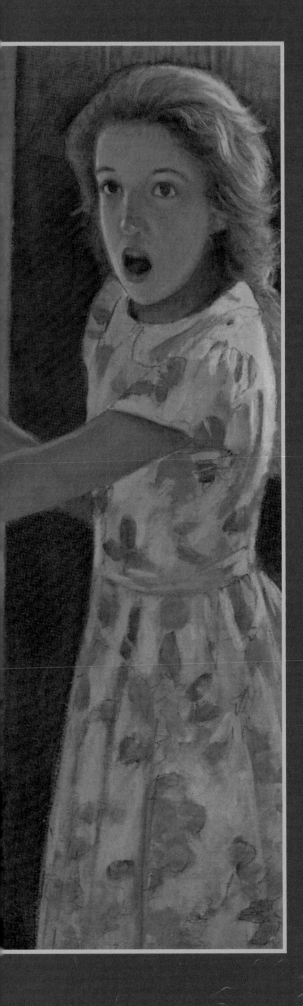

The next morning Leah forced open the heavy barn doors to start her chores. A loud whinny greeted her. Leah ran and hugged the familiar furry neck and kissed the white snip of a nose. "You're back!" she cried. "How did you get here?"

Then Leah noticed the note tied to her pony's halter:

Dear Leah,

This is the finest pony in the county. But he's a little bit small for me and a little bit big for my grandson. He fits you much better.

Your friend,

Mr. B.

P.S. I heard how you saved your family's farm. These hard times won't last forever.

And they didn't.

Leah's Pony

Meet the Author

Elizabeth Friedrich has written many books. One of her books has sold more than a half-million copies. Friedrich likes to write books about family activities and values, as she does in "Leah's Pony." Currently she lives in New Hampshire in a 150-year-old farmhouse with her husband, children, sheep, and a horse named Tuffy.

Meet the Illustrator

Michael Garland is an artist who does many different kinds of work. He is a layout designer, a portrait painter, and an advertising artist. The faces Michael Garland draws look almost like photographs. Michael Garland is a talented still life and landscape painter, too.

Theme Connections

Within the Selection

Record your answers to the questions below in the Response Journal section of your Writer's Notebook. In small groups, report the ideas you wrote. Discuss your ideas with the rest of the group. Then choose a person to report your group's answers to the class.

- When Leah's father bought her pony, the family was living a comfortable country life. Why did times become hard when the corn did not grow?
- How did Leah save her family's farm and the country life they loved?

Across Selections

- What role did the weather play in "Heartland" and in "Leah's Pony"?

Beyond the Selection

- Have you ever given up something that you loved in order to help your family or a friend?
- Think about how "Leah's Pony" adds to what you know about country life.
- Add items to the Concept/Question Board about country life.

The Birthplace of Herbert Hoover, West Branch, Iowa. 1931. **Grant Wood.** Oil on composition board. $29 \frac{5}{8} \times 39 \frac{3}{4}$ in. The Minneapolis Institute of Arts, Minneapolis, Minnesota. ©2001 Estate of Grant Wood/Licensed by VAGA, New York, NY.

Country Store, Alabama. 1936. **Walker Evans.** Silver gelatin print. Library of Congress.

July Hay. 1943. **Thomas Hart Benton.**
Oil and egg tempera on composition board.
38" × 26$\frac{3}{4}$". The Metropolitan Museum of Art,
New York. ©2001 Thomas H. Benton and Rita P.
Benton Testamentary Trusts/Licensed by VAGA,
New York, NY.

Calhoun. 1955. **Grandma Moses (Anna Mary
Robertson Moses).** Oil on pressed wood. 16$\frac{3}{4}$"
× 24". The National Museum of Women in the Arts,
Washington, DC. Copyright ©1986, Grandma Moses
Properties Co., New York.

Cows in the Parlor

A Visit to a Dairy Farm

by Cynthia McFarland

Every day is a busy day on Clear Creek Farm. Winter, spring, summer, and fall, the cows on the dairy farm must be milked—twice a day, every day.

When the snow is deep in the fields, and when the hot summer sun shines down on the pastures, the cows need to be milked. Even on holidays, Charlie Riddle, the farmer, must milk his cows. A dairy cow doesn't have a day off.

Maggie is a Jersey cow. Jerseys are always tan or brown. Some have white spots on their faces and bodies. They are friendly cows and like to be petted.

There are fifty cows on Clear Creek Farm, where Maggie lives. Fancy, Belle, Heather, and Sparkle are some of the other cows' names. It is not easy to think of names for fifty cows.

A tag with a number hangs from the chain around Maggie's neck. Another tag is attached to her ear. When a farmer has many cows, he needs a way to keep track of them. The numbers on the tags help him do this. The neck chains jingle and rattle when the cows walk or shake their heads.

When the wind is blowing and it is raining or snowing, the cows stay inside the barn. The straw makes a cozy bed when it is cold outside.

When the weather is nice, the cows like to graze in the pasture. The sunshine is warm on Maggie's back as she rests after eating. In the spring and summer when the nights are warmer, the cows sleep outside in the cool grass.

A cow doesn't have top teeth at the front of her mouth as a horse, a dog, or a person does. Maggie has a very long, rough tongue. By wrapping it around the tall grass she can pull off a bite and then chew the grass with her strong back teeth.

In the summer, Mr. Riddle and the farm workers cut grass, dry it in the sun, and make it into bales of hay. The cows will have hay to eat when the grass in the pasture is brown and dry in the winter.

But a cow needs more than grass and hay to make good milk. Charlie Riddle also makes feed from the corn that was planted in the spring. Machines chop the whole cornstalk into small pieces.

Then the silo is filled with this chopped corn, which is called *silage*. The silo is very tall. It can hold enough silage to feed the farmer's cows for many months. When snow covers the cornfields, there will still be food for the cows in the silo.

The cows eat their silage at a long trough, called a bunk. Mr. Riddle uses a tractor and feed wagon to take the silage from the silo to the bunk, where the cows are waiting to eat. The cows moo when they see the tractor because they know that soon they will be fed.

Maggie and the other cows know when it is time to be milked because Charlie Riddle and the farm workers milk them at the same time every day. If the cows are out in the field, they start walking up to the barn gate at milking time.

Early in the morning, when most people are asleep in their warm beds, the cows are being milked. In the evening, when most people sit down to eat dinner, the cows must be milked again. At Clear Creek Farm, the Riddle family eats supper earlier in the afternoon, or after the evening milking is finished.

The parlor in a dairy barn is not a pretty living room. It is the room where the cows are milked.

When Maggie comes into the parlor, her udder is firm and full of milk. She stands in a small pen, or stanchion, and the gates are closed so that she can't leave until she has been milked. Every time she is milked, her udder is cleaned and all the dirt is washed off.

Farmers used to milk their cows by hand into a bucket. That took a long time. Now there are automatic milking machines to make the job quicker and easier.

The milking machines don't hurt the cows. Suction from the machines gently pulls the milk from the cows.

The milk runs through shiny silver pipes into a large tank. There the milk is kept cold until it is picked up by the milk hauler.

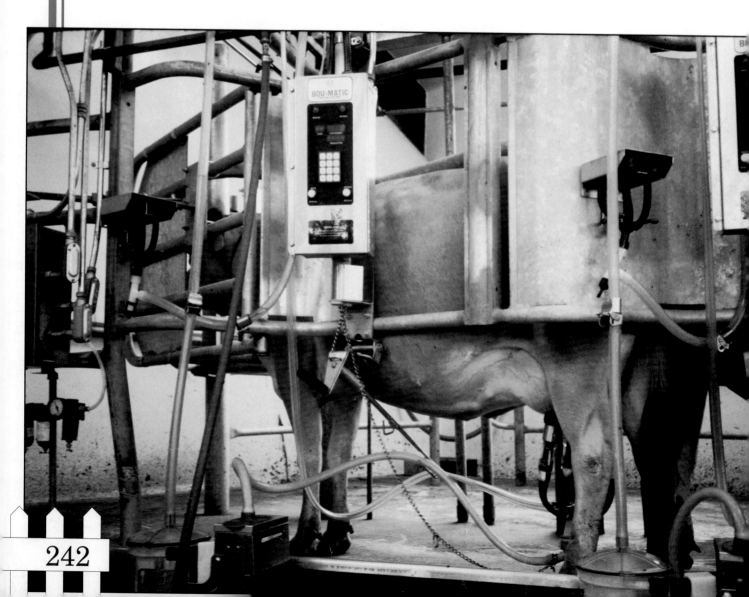

When the hauler comes, he pumps all the milk into his long tanker truck and takes it to the creamery. There the milk is made into butter, cheese, ice cream, and yogurt. It is also put into cartons so people can pour a glass to drink or have some on their cereal for breakfast. In one day a single cow can give enough milk to fill more than fifty glasses.

To keep making milk, a cow must have a baby every year. Cats and dogs have several babies at a time. A cow usually has only one.

Maggie has just had a calf. The calf is sweet and brown, with large dark eyes like a deer's.

The calf nurses from her mother. That first milk is very important to the baby. It is rich with extra vitamins to keep the newborn calf from getting sick.

After the calf has been with her a day, Maggie will go back into the milking herd. Her calf will live with all the other babies. Each calf has her own small pen bedded with fresh, sweet-smelling straw. Mr. Riddle feeds them milk from a bottle, and they learn to eat grain from a bucket.

A calf is soft and warm and will suck on the farmer's finger, trying to find milk. She calls *"maaa maaa"* at feeding time.

Calves are frisky and like to play. After running and jumping, they take naps in the sunshine.

A female calf is called a heifer. A male calf is called a bull calf. Charlie Riddle keeps the heifer. Sometimes he sells the bull calves so another farmer can raise them.

Maggie's calf is a heifer. In two years she will be old enough to be bred and have a baby of her own. After she calves, she will be called a cow and will become part of the milking herd just like her mother, Maggie.

After the evening milking, Mr. Riddle finishes his chores. When the parlor is clean, the milking machines and pipes are washed, and the cows are fed, his day's work is done.

The cows finish eating their dinner and lie down to sleep. Soon bright stars glitter in the night sky above the quiet, dark pastures.

When the morning sun comes up again, another busy day will already have begun on Clear Creek Farm.

Cows in the Parlor

A Visit to a Dairy Farm

Meet the Author

Cynthia McFarland always dreamed of living on a farm. Since graduating from college, she has lived on beef and dairy farms in Ohio, Florida, and South Carolina. Her books *Cows in the Parlor* and *Hoofbeats* illustrate some of the adventures of living on a farm. She was the photographer, as well as the author, of *Hoofbeats*. Cynthia says that writing and photographing the book has *"brought home, once again, the sheer delight and beauty of the horse, and of that unique communion between the animal and those who work with him."* Cynthia lives on a farm in Florida with her horses, sheep, cats, and dogs.

Theme Connections

Within the Selection

Record your answers to the questions below in the Response Journal section of your Writer's Notebook. In small groups, report the ideas you wrote. Discuss your ideas with the rest of the group. Then choose a person to report your group's answers to the class.

- What are some ways that country life on Clear Creek Farm is different from life in the city?
- How has technology helped make the dairy farmer's life easier?
- What kinds of products come from dairy farms like Clear Creek Farm?

Across Selections

- How does "Cows in the Parlor" remind you of "Heartland"?

Beyond the Selection

- Think about how "Cows in the Parlor" adds to what you know about country life.
- Add items to the Concept/Question Board about country life.

Focus Questions What do farmworkers do?
How does the labor of farmworkers affect everyone's lives?

Farmworkers

Alma Flor Ada
translated by Rosa Zubizarreta
illustrated by Simón Silva

Farmworkers nombre en inglés
para el pueblo campesino,
trabajadores del campo,
bajo un mismo cielo unidos.

Gracias te doy, campesino,
por los frutos de tus manos
creceré en fuerza y bondad
comiendo lo que has sembrado.

Farmworkers is the name we give
to the people who work the land,
who harvest the fields,
united beneath one sky.

Thank you, farmworker,
for the fruits your hands have brought me.
I will grow stronger and kinder
as I eat what you have grown.

Focus Questions Many people and conditions are responsible for supplying a country's food. Who and what are some of these people and conditions? Why does it take a combination of things to meet a country's needs?

Thanks

Alma Flor Ada
translated by Rosa Zubizarreta
illustrated by Simón Silva

Gracias

Aire y cielo, lluvia y sol,
nube y sombra, campo y flor.
Gracias, tierra, por tus frutos
de delicioso sabor.

Thanks

Wind and sky, rain and sun,
cloud and shade, field and flower.
Thank you, Earth,
for all of your delicious fruits.

Focus Questions Why is it sometimes difficult to follow the rules? Although rules are important, sometimes there are good reasons for breaking rules. What might some of these good reasons be?

Just Plain Fancy

by Patricia Polacco

Kaleb and his two daughters hurried along Lancaster County Road in their buggy. Cars whizzed by them, but they paid no mind. *Clop, clop, clop* went the horse's hooves on the pavement.

"Papa," Naomi asked, "why don't we have a car like the English?"

"It is not our way, child. We are in no hurry," he said as he drew up the reins and slowly directed the horse into their farmyard.

250 🌸

While their father unharnessed and watered the horse, Naomi and Ruth skipped toward the henhouse. The chickens were Naomi's responsibility. She saw to their feeding and watering as well as the collecting of their eggs.

"Everything around here is so plain," Naomi complained. "Our clothes are plain, our houses are plain, even our chickens are plain. It would pleasure me—just once—to have something fancy."

"Shaw, Nomi, you aughtn't to be saying such things," little Ruth scolded.

As Naomi and Ruth searched the field for eggs laid outside the henhouse, they spotted a very unusual one nestled in the tall grass down the drive and behind the henhouse, next to the road.

"This egg looks different from any I have ever seen," Naomi said quietly. "It's still warm—let's put it in Henny's nest. This one needs to be hatched." She gently picked up the egg and eased it into her basket.

Although it was a little bigger than Henny's other eggs and a little darker in color, Naomi gently tucked the egg into the nest while Henny and Ruth looked on.

"You're so good with chickens," Ruth chirped. "I just know you're going to get your white cap this year. Momma says you're ready."

Naomi was proud of her chickens and the way she raised them. The elders were coming for a working bee, or frolic, in the coming summer. And Naomi wondered whether her parents might present her with the white cap on that day. Her thoughts were interrupted by Ruth's voice.

"Ain't we pleasured," she said. "You wanted something fancy, and now you've got it."

As the days passed, Naomi and Ruth checked Henny's nest constantly. Every day they peered over the edge of the crib, watching for signs of cracks in the shells. Then, one day, the eggs hatched.

"Look at the little chick from the fancy egg, Nomi," Ruth squealed.

"That egg was fancy inside and out, wasn't it?" said Naomi. "Fancy. That's just what we'll name this chick."

"Fancy, Fancy, Fancy, Fancy," Ruth sang out as she jumped about. Naomi smiled and clapped her hands.

All that afternoon, the girls stayed with Henny, watching and studying their special little chick.

Weeks passed. Henny's chicks grew quickly and were soon scratching around in the dirt. They had all lost their yellow down feathers and had grown bright white ones. All of them, except Fancy. Fancy looked very different from the others. There was no doubt about it——this chick wasn't plain!

One afternoon in the washhouse, Naomi and Ruth overheard Aunt Sarai talking to cousin Hannah about a person in the neighboring Amish community.

"She dressed too fancy," Sarai said. "She had to be *shunned*!"

"Is it wrong to be fancy?" Naomi asked.

"Indeed, yes!" snapped Hannah. "We are plain folk. It is in our laws, the *Ordnung,* that we must be plain!"

"What does . . . 'shun' mean?" Ruth asked haltingly.

"Someone who is shunned is shamed in front of the elders. After that, friends and neighbors are instructed not to speak to that person. They are no longer one of us," Sarai answered with authority. Naomi and Ruth looked at each other and hurried outside to hang up the washing. Naomi felt botherment inside.

As soon as they were finished, the girls ran to the henhouse.

"What are we going to do?" Ruth asked. "Fancy is too fancy to be Amish!" Then Fancy ruffled up his feathers and did something that took their breath clean away.

"We'll have to hide him until we know what to do," Naomi said finally. "The elders will be here for the frolic tomorrow."

"He'll be shunned," Ruth whimpered. "Maybe we will be, too!"

They put Fancy into another part of the henhouse and locked the door.

The next morning, the neighboring Amish folk
arrived for the frolic. The men and boys helped add
a stable onto the Vleckes' barn. They worked hard in
the sun while the womenfolk cooked and gossiped.
Naomi and Ruth helped serve the food, pour
lemonade, and thread needles for the women who
were quilting. This should have been a happy day
for them. But the girls were not pleasured because
they were sad with worry about Fancy.

When she had served the last ladle of lemonade,
Naomi started toward the henhouse. Just then she
noticed the open door. But before she could get
there to shut it, Fancy darted out and ran toward
the gathering, flapping his wings.

"Oh, no!" Naomi called out. "This is all my fault.
I wanted something fancy. I should have known
better than to make that kind of wish!"

257

Tears ran down Ruth's cheeks when she saw what had happened. "Poooor Fancy," she cried. "Now he'll be shunned."

Over . . . Under . . . Around . . . Through. . . . Naomi ran after Fancy, trying to catch him before anyone noticed. And that's about the time that Fancy decided to head straight for the elders. He flew at Martha, the oldest member of the gathering. Adjusting her glasses, she gasped as he flew over her head just before landing on the clothesline where the quilts were airing.

"Please don't shun him," Naomi cried. "I did this! I made him fancy," she sobbed. At that moment, pleased with all the attention, Fancy ruffled his feathers and did for the guests what he had done for the girls in the henhouse the day before. Those who weren't speechless were stunned!

"Dry your tears, child." It was Martha who finally spoke. "This isn't your doing. This be God's handiwork. Only He could think up colors like that."

"You mean you aren't going to shun him?" Ruth asked.

"One can only be shunned for going against the ways of our people," Martha continued. "This is no plain old chicken. This be one of God's most beautiful creations. He is fancy, child, and that's the way of it."

All who were gathered there rejoiced in Fancy's beauty. "I believe you have this coming, child," old Martha said as she held out the new white organdy cap. "Your family believes you have earned this well. And I agree. Not only have you given good and faithful care to your flock of chickens, but you have also raised one of the finest peacocks I ever did see!"

Standing proudly amidst the gathering, Naomi held Fancy in her arms. She had learned many things that day.

And although no one ever quite knew how Fancy came to be hatched by Henny, it was never questioned. Plainly it was a miracle . . . and sometimes miracles are JUST PLAIN FANCY!

Just Plain Fancy

Meet the Author and Illustrator

Patricia Polacco had fond feelings about her family, whom she describes as marvelous storytellers. She says, *"My fondest memories are of sitting around a stove or open fire, eating apples and popping corn while listening to the old ones tell glorious stories about the past. . . . With each retelling our stories gained a little more oomph!"* Polacco had difficulty reading as a child, but was admired for her ability to draw. She is now very well known as both an author and an illustrator.

Theme Connections

Within the Selection

Record your answers to the questions below in the Response Journal section of your Writer's Notebook. In small groups, report the ideas you wrote. Discuss your ideas with the rest of the group. Then choose a person to report your group's answers to the class.

- Naomi and Ruth were Amish children. What did they think made their country life plain?
- Why did Naomi name the chick Fancy?

Across Selections

- How is this story like the other selections you have read?
- How are Naomi and Ruth like Leah in "Leah's Pony"? How are they different?

Beyond the Selection

- Think about how "Just Plain Fancy" adds to what you know about country life.
- Add items to the Concept/Question Board about country life.

261

Focus Questions Compare the advantages of small, family farms to big, company farms. What are some of the disadvantages? How can small farms compete with big farms?

What Ever Happened to the Baxter Place?

Pat Ross
illustrated by Roger Duvoisin

Some years ago you could turn off the main road outside a small town in Maryland onto a dirt road which stretched three miles. The old dirt road was called Flatland Road, and it led you straight to the Baxter Place.

It was really a farm belonging to the Baxter family—acres and acres of fields and meadows and woodland—but everybody around just called it the Baxter Place.

A herd of cows grazed in the east meadow. Wild ducks and geese swam in the pond nearby.

Stretching up to a big white farmhouse was a field of soybeans, making a pretty blanket of green in the spring and summer months.

The Baxter Place spread out over nearly three hundred acres. The south field—the biggest and flattest—was planted in rotation with corn one year and barley the next. The rolling east field was well-suited for alfalfa, giving three cuttings each year. The west field, the smallest stretch, was reserved for crops the Baxters might want for their own, with surplus going for sale.

The fields were divided by woods, like nature's markers.

There were four in the family. Sara Baxter was a big, strong woman with a friendly way, and Pete Baxter was a tall and wiry man with skin toughened and tanned from being outdoors all year round. Sue Ann, the older child, seemed to take after her mother's side of the family. Last there was young Pete, named after his dad, but everybody called him Pee Wee. It's said he was so tiny when he was born that he fit in a shoe box, so Pee Wee they called him, and the name stuck.

The Baxter Place was a business—a farm business. It was also a way of life.

Nothing kept Pete Baxter from the work in the fields or in the big dairy barn that had milking stalls for twenty cows at a time. Pete knew every crop, every one of their hundred cows by name, and everything that happened on the farm. For him, farming was more than any regular full-time job, and he liked being outdoors every day all year round.

Sara Baxter raised chickens in a chicken house. During the laying season, she collected about a hundred eggs every day, then drove them to town to Hammil's Country Market to be sold. She also grew vegetables, and those that didn't get eaten right away got canned and

preserved for the long winter or taken to the market along with the eggs. Sara kept careful records of everything that was bought or sold for the farm. She was not only the farm's bookkeeper but also the business-minded one in the family.

Jim and Wally were the hired hands—farmers who work at farming other people's land. Jim was a crackerjack repairman when the tractor and equipment broke down—which was more often than he liked. And Wally knew the planting seasons like the back of his hand. Folks said he could smell a late spring frost in the air. Both Jim and Wally came every morning at six sharp and often stayed till late in the evening. They had worked with Pete for fifteen years.

Sue Ann did her chores every morning before the school bus came up Flatland Road. She cleaned the calves' stalls, fed the chickens, helped with the milking, and set the table for breakfast—which came *after* chores.

Pee Wee, being younger, got away with a little less in the way of work. He was in charge of feeding the three big watchdogs and an untold number of cats, cleaning the chicken house, and helping Sara set out breakfast for everyone.

All the folks around those parts said the Baxter Place was the prettiest, neatest farm they'd ever seen, and the Baxters were some of the nicest folks they knew. Luckiest, too. And they were right—until the day the man from the market stopped by.

Jess Hammil owned the farmers' market where Sara took her eggs and produce to be sold. Sara, Pete, and Jess had all been in grade school together, so they went way back. Jess came to see the Baxters the day he learned the lease on his small vegetable market in town wasn't going to be renewed. A fancy new building was going up in its place, and he sure couldn't afford those rents.

Now, he figured if he could buy his own land—and not rent—something like this wasn't likely to happen again. He had saved the cash, so maybe the Baxters would be willing to part with that small west field. With those twenty-five acres, Jess could not only have his market, he could also grow much of his own seasonal produce instead of always depending on other farmers. The field was right off the main road from town, so people would be likely to stop and buy.

It was true that particular piece of land was what you might call extra. Sara and Pete had always thought they would save it for Sue Ann and Pee Wee. But Sue Ann was headed for forestry college in a year and planned to move later on to the mountains where her work would be. And Pee Wee, young as he was, had his

heart set on being a mathematician, and claimed he was allergic to field work—which certainly seemed to be true!

Jess's being an old friend and all helped the Baxters decide to sell. Also, Sara thought it would be kind of nice to have a market for her sales so close by. They shook hands and made a deal.

Within a year, Jess opened a brand-new market. He planted his land with seasonal produce crops. When word got around that the state was planning to widen and resurface Main Road, Jess knew this meant even more business for him.

Pete and Sara figured they'd not only made some money to pay the bills more easily, but they'd also done a favor for a friend.

Every year for the past five, Emma Price from Homestead Realty Company had made her call on the Baxters. Every year it was the same: Emma's real estate company was interested in purchasing and developing their meadow and woodland area around the pond. Would they consider selling? The offer would be handsome.

Every year they greeted Emma Price politely, but their answer had always been a firm no. They needed the meadow for the cows. And how could they part with the woods and pond? Besides, they didn't need the money. So each year they bade Emma good-by with the same answer.

But one year, things were a little different. The corn harvest that fall had been a total loss. There had been too much rain during planting time and a dry spell just when they needed rain. Corn was their livelihood, and without the crop's sale the bills would go unpaid. Sara figured they could barely pay for the farm's necessities that year. They also owed the bank a mortgage on the house and the land plus money they had borrowed for seed and a new tractor.

They insisted they would not part with the meadow, pond, and woods. Still, they didn't like getting into debt any more if they could help it. Would the Homestead Realty Company consider the rolling east field? they asked. Emma Price was pleasantly surprised and said yes right away.

It was the toughest decision they'd ever had to make together.

Would the company please save some of the trees when they made room for houses? Sue Ann asked. Emma Price assured her they'd make every effort to do just that. Would the Baxters get the best price, even though the east field was the company's second choice? Sara and Pete asked. Emma quoted them a price. Would the new people have children his age? Pee Wee asked. Everyone laughed nervously. Pete quickly figured out loud that they could use the front soybean field for alfalfa, too. There would just be less of a soybean crop, and they would have to sell off some of the older cows in the herd, but the fifty milk-producing cows would not go hungry.

Hurting with the pain of parting with their good land, but having to, the Baxters signed the east field over to Emma Price's company. Homestead Realty paid them without delay. In turn, the Baxters paid for their bad year and looked forward to better ones.

Soon bulldozers were clearing the land, leaving pitifully few of the trees, going against what Emma Price had promised. But it was not all bad, the Baxters told themselves and each other. When the noises and smells of building began to die down, the new houses looked pretty and comfortable, and the people who moved into them seemed friendly enough. It was just strange to see the old alfalfa field planted with so many houses.

Several years of good crops did follow and things seemed to be almost back to normal, even though more and more houses were being built all around. Sue Ann won a partial scholarship to forestry college. Everybody was proud of her, but missed her a lot.

Pee Wee had just started high school when the milking problem came up. Each morning

he'd pitch in to take Sue Ann's place. Jim and Wally still arrived at the crack of dawn, but Jim was getting on in years, and it seemed to take him longer to get the cows milked than it used to. Besides, a lot of the local farmers were putting in new automatic equipment—milking parlors, they called them, with an elevated stall for each cow and tubes leading right to the main tank. The Baxters still relied on the old methods. Not that they wouldn't have changed over. But the cost of the new setup was more than they could swing. So, for a while at least, Pee Wee did his best to help out. Wally never missed a day, but he was no longer up to heavy work, so Sara pitched in more often.

Still, it got harder and harder to compete with the milk production of neighboring farmers who had installed milking parlors to handle larger herds in less time than it took the Baxters. Milk sales were barely bringing in enough to cover costs, so it wasn't long before the Baxters began to sell off the rest of their herd.

Finally, only five cows grazed in the meadow. The milking barn was practically empty. And even though the Baxters didn't have their herd, they took comfort in knowing that the milk and butter on their kitchen table was not store-bought, but still their own.

The following spring George Stillwell came to see Pete and Sara Baxter about using the pond and meadow area for sports land. He didn't want to *buy* the land—which pleased the Baxters, as they'd made up their minds they'd never part with the pond. George Stillwell proposed leasing

the area for eight years. He would put up what he called a "rustic cabin" and, in turn, rent it out to hunters during the fall and winter gunning seasons.

Pete figured that was a good enough deal. The pond was a safe distance from the housing development. Besides, the whole area filled up with hunters during the duck and goose seasons anyway. The Baxters had always let some hunters on their land, so a few more couldn't do much harm, except for the noise. And without actually giving up the land, they would be paid for it. This would fill the hole in their pockets left by the loss of milk money, and would help to fill Pee Wee's college savings account. So Sara, too, reluctantly agreed.

In the next year, the cabin, only a little bigger than the Baxters had expected, went up. They could live with a few hunters for eight years.

Pee Wee, now Petie to everyone except his family, went off to engineering school a whole year ahead of his graduating class. This came as no great surprise to the Baxters, and his ambitions made them proud.

Jim retired officially, but still came around to tinker with the machinery and complain how the new tractor wasn't up to the old model.

Again, things returned almost to normal. Pete and Sara had a smaller place, but it was plenty for them and Wally to handle. They still had the big south field for corn and barley, and the front field for other crops. Sara had her chickens and her garden. Life on the farm was different, what with the changes and Sue Ann and Pee Wee away most of the year. Perhaps now things would stay put for a while. And they did in fact—for some time.

But things once set out of order never quite stay put for long.

One day something happened that the Baxters found hard to understand. Jess Hammil sold out to a developer, a big developer.

Jess's country market and his land were bulldozed to make Main Shopping Mall, featuring a giant supermarket, a discount drugstore, a dress boutique, a chain department store, and countless other small shops.

Not long after this, Homestead Realty Company made the Baxters an offer on the big south field. This time they didn't *have* to sell, but Wally was about to retire and Pete and Sara were no longer up to heavy work. They could look for new hired hands, but it just didn't seem the same. The offer was tempting, so they finally accepted.

One thing led to another. The man who'd rented the pond made an offer to buy now that the lease was about to expire. Since the pond and meadow would never be the same again, what with a shopping center bordering it, the Baxters could see little reason to hold onto it. It had lost almost all its meaning for them.

After the sale to George Stillwell—the most profitable and the most heartbreaking for the Baxters—the cabin was turned into Rustic Manor Motor Lodge and Tennis Club almost overnight.

The Baxter Place was not even half of what it had been not too many years before. But the trees—those that were left—still acted as dividers, trying hard to keep the Baxter Place separate.

Sara and Pete still had the front field leading up to the old farmhouse. In the early years, they had had to struggle hard just to make the place pay for itself. Now they had some money in the bank. That was something.

Folks couldn't still say the Baxter Place was the prettiest, neatest place around—not the way it had gotten so divided up and changed. But folks could still say the Baxters were some of the nicest folks they'd ever known. And they were. That had not changed. But so many things *had*.

"What ever happened to the old Baxter Place?" somebody asked. And nobody could quite say. Not even the Baxters.

What Ever Happened to the Baxter Place?

Meet the Author

Pat Ross began a career in publishing at Humpty Dumpty's Magazine. As she edited children's books, she discovered her own voice for writing. Many of her books focus on the spirit and challenges of young girls. Her book *M and M and the Big Bag* was named a Children's Choice Book by the International Reading Association and the Children's Book Council.

Meet the Illustrator

Roger Duvoisin was an author as well as an illustrator. He was born in Geneva, Switzerland, and became a citizen of the United States in 1938. Throughout his career, he wrote over 40 children's books and illustrated more than 140. Roger is well-known for his animal fables. He had a talent for bringing animals to life through both his words and his drawings. He won numerous awards as an author and illustrator. He is perhaps best known for the *Happy Lion* series in which he was the illustrator and his wife, Louise Fatio, was the author.

Theme Connections

Within the Selection

Record your answers to the questions below in the Response Journal section of your Writer's Notebook. In small groups, report the ideas you wrote. Discuss your ideas with the rest of the group. Then choose a person to report your group's answers to the class.

- What made the Baxter Place special?
- How did technology affect country life at the Baxter Place?
- Why couldn't anyone answer the question, "What ever happened to the old Baxter Place?"

Across Selections

- How are the Baxters like Leah's family in "Leah's Pony"?
- How was Clear Creek Farm in "Cows in the Parlor" different from the Baxter Place?

Beyond the Selection

- Think about how "What Ever Happened to the Baxter Place?" adds to what you know about country life.
- Add items to the Concept/Question Board about country life.

If you're not from the prairie . . .

David Bouchard
illustrated by Henry Ripplinger

If you're not from the prairie,
You don't know the sun,
You *can't* know the sun.

Diamonds that bounce off crisp winter snow,
Warm waters in dugouts and lakes that we know.
The sun is our friend from when we are young,
A child of the prairie is part of the sun.

If you're not from the prairie,
You *don't* know the sun.

If you're not from the prairie,
You don't know the wind,
You *can't* know the wind.

Our cold winds of winter cut right to the core,
Hot summer wind devils can blow down the door.
As children we know when we play any game,
The wind will be there, yet we play just the same.

If you're not from the prairie,
You *don't* know the wind.

If you're not from the prairie,
You don't know the sky,
You *can't* know the sky.

     The bold prairie sky is clear, bright and blue,
     Though sometimes cloud messages give us a clue.
     Monstrous grey mushrooms can hint of a storm,
     Or painted pink feathers say goodbye to the warm.

          If you're not from the prairie,
          You *don't* know the sky.

If you're not from the prairie,
You don't know what's flat,
You've *never* seen flat.

When travellers pass through across our great plain,
They all view our home, they all say the same:
"It's simple and flat!" They've not learned to see,
The particular beauty that's now part of me.

If you're not from the prairie,
You *don't* know what's flat.

If you're not from the prairie,
You've not heard the grass,
You've never *heard* grass.

In strong summer winds, the grains and grass bend
And sway to a dance that seems never to end.
It whispers its secrets—they tell of this land
And the rhythm of life played by nature's own hand.

If you're not from the prairie,
You've never *heard* grass.

So you're not from the prairie,
And yet you know snow.
You *think* you know snow?

Blizzards bring danger, as legends have told,
In deep drifts we roughhouse, ignoring the cold.
At times we look out at great seas of white,
So bright is the sun that we squeeze our eyes tight.

If you're not from the prairie,
You *don't* know snow.

289

If you're not from the prairie,
You don't know our trees,
You *can't* know our trees.

   The trees that we know have taken so long,
   To live through our seasons, to grow tall
      and strong.
   They're loved and they're treasured, we watched
      as they grew,
   We knew they were special—the prairie has few.

      If you're not from the prairie,
      You *don't* know our trees.

Still, you're not from the prairie,
And yet you know cold. . . .
You say you've *been* cold?

Of all of those memories we share when we're old,
None are more clear than that hard bitter cold.
You'll not find among us a soul who can say:
"I've conquered the wind on a cold winter's day."

If you're not from the prairie,
You *don't* know the cold.
You've *never* been cold!

If you're not from the prairie,
You don't know me.
You just can't know *ME*.

  You see,
  My hair's mostly wind,
  My eyes filled with grit,
  My skin's red or brown,
  My lips chapped and split.

    I've lain on the prairie and heard grasses sigh.
    I've stared at the vast open bowl of the sky.
    I've seen all those castles and faces in clouds,
    My home is the prairie, and I cry out loud.

If you're not from the prairie, you can't know my soul,
You don't know our blizzards, you've not fought our cold.
You can't know my mind, nor ever my heart,
Unless deep within you, there's somehow a part. . . .
A part of these things that I've said that I know,
The wind, sky and earth, the storms and the snow.
Best say you have—and then we'll be one,
For we will have shared that same blazing sun.

If you're not from the prairie . . .

Meet the Author

David Bouchard did not want to be a writer when he was in school. Instead, he sang in the choir and played sports. He started his career as a teacher and a principal. When Bouchard was 27, he began reading a lot and ten years later, he began writing children's books. He travels to schools, speaking to students about poetry and the importance of rhythm and the music of words. He has five children and many pets, including an Amazon parrot. Bouchard lives in Victoria, a city in British Columbia, Canada.

Meet the Illustrator

Henry Ripplinger was born and raised on the prairies of Saskatchewan, Canada. Ripplinger began painting while he was a high school teacher in 1969. He values the beauty of the world around us and wants to capture it in his paintings. He says, *"It is my hope to confront the viewer of my paintings with the uniqueness and beauty that is always present in our environment."* When asked to give advice to aspiring artists, Ripplinger says that discipline, commitment, and desire are most important. He owns his own fine arts gallery in Regina, Canada.

Theme Connections

Within the Selection

Record your answers to the questions below in the Response Journal section of your Writer's Notebook. In small groups, report the ideas you wrote. Discuss your ideas with the rest of the group. Then choose a person to report your group's answers to the class.

- What is special about life on the prairie?
- Why does the author say that there are so many things you *can't* know if you're not from the prairie?

Across Selections

- Compare how "Heartland" and "If you're not from the prairie…" tell about country life.

Beyond the Selection

- What is special about where you live? Would someone from far away be able to *know* it in the same way you do?
- Think about how "If you're not from the prairie…" adds to what you know about country life.
- Add items to the Concept/Question Board about country life.

Pronunciation Key

a as in **a**t

ā as in l**a**te

â as in c**a**re

ä as in f**a**ther

e as in s**e**t

ē as in m**e**

i as in **i**t

ī as in k**i**te

o as in **o**x

ō as in r**o**se

ô as in b**ou**ght and r**a**w

oi as in c**oi**n

o͝o as in b**oo**k

o͞o as in t**oo**

or as in f**or**m

ou as in **ou**t

u as in **u**p

ū as in **u**se

ûr as in t**ur**n; g**er**m, l**ear**n, f**ir**m, w**or**k

ə as in **a**bout, chick**e**n, penc**i**l, cann**o**n, circ**u**s

ch as in **ch**air

hw as in **wh**ich

ng as in ri**ng**

sh as in **sh**op

th as in **th**in

t͟h as in **th**ere

zh as in trea**s**ure

The mark (ʹ) is placed after a syllable with a heavy accent, as in **chicken** (**chik**ʹ ən).

The mark (ʹ) after a syllable shows a lighter accent, as in **disappear** (**dis**ʹ ə pērʹ).

Glossary

A

absolutely (ab´ sə lōōt´ lē) *adv.* Certainly; for sure.

advise (əd vīz´) *v.* To give information.

adze (adz) *n.* A tool shaped like an axe. It is used by the **Tsimshian** tribe to create a pattern on the surface of a wood carving. The adze handle is handmade from the elbow of a yew or alder branch. The blade is made of steel.

allergic (ə lûr´ jik) *adj.* Having an unpleasant reaction to certain things.

ambition (am bi´ shən) *n.* A strong desire for success.

amidst (ə midst´) *prep.* In the middle of.

analyze (an´ l īz´) *v.* To examine the parts of something.

ancestor (an´ ses tər) *n.* A parent, grandparent, great-grandparent, and so on.

artificial (är´ tə fish´ əl) *adj.* Made by people rather than nature.

auction (ôk´ shôn) *n.* A public sale where each item is sold to the person who will pay the highest price.

automatic (ô tə ma´ tik) *adj.* Operating by itself.

away (ə wā´) *v.* To go somewhere.

B

babushka (bə bōōsh´ kə) *n.* A head scarf shaped like a triangle.

bale (bāl) *n.* A large bundle of hay, packed tightly and tied together.

banquet (bang´ kwit) *n.* A feast; a large dinner.

befriend (bi frend´) *v.* To become friends with.

blacksmith (blak´ smith´) *n.* A person who makes horseshoes.

boisterous (boi´ stə rəs) *adj.* Lively and noisy.

bold (bōld) *adj.* Very easy to see; standing out clearly.

bolt (bōlt) *n.* A roll of cloth.

bosom (bōōz´ əm) *n.* The chest; the heart.

botherment (both´ ər mənt) *n.* A feeling of worry.

297

bough (bou) *n.* One of the major branches of a tree.

bouquet (boo´ kā) *n.* A bunch of flowers.

boutique (boo tēk´) *n.* A small shop.

bowie knife (bō´ ē nīf´) *n.* A thick-handled knife named for James Bowie.

brandish (bran´ dish) *v.* To swing or shake an object in a way that signals possible danger.

brave (brāv) *adj.* Having courage.

britches (brich´ iz) *n.* Breeches; pants; trousers.

bronco (brong´ kō) *n.* A wild horse.

buckboard (buk´ bord´) *n.* A horse-drawn carriage made from a long, wooden board or simple frame.

bugler (bū´ glər) *n.* A person who plays the bugle or trumpet.

butternut (bə´ tər nət´) *n.* A type of sweet nut that comes from a tree in the walnut family and can be eaten.

C

calabash (kal´ ə bash´) *n.* The shell of a dried gourd, used as a bowl.

card (kärd) *v.* To comb wool.

cater (ka´ tər) *v.* To prepare and serve food for a private occasion.

challah (hä´ lə) *n.* A bread, which is often braided, made with eggs. Challah is eaten on the Jewish Sabbath.

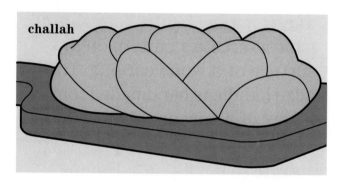

challah

charity (châr´ ə tē) *n.* 1. A group that gives help to the needy and operates without making any money. 2. Generosity and helpfulness.

chore (chor) *n.* A small job done regularly.

circulation (sər´ kyə lā´ shən) *n.* Movement around many different places or people.

clan (klan) *n.* A group of families with one common ancestor. The **Tsimshian** have four major clans: the Eagles, Wolves, Ravens, and Killer Whales.

clench (klench) *v.* To close the teeth or fingers tightly.

cobbler (kob´ lər) *n.* A person who repairs shoes and boots.

coffin (kô´ fin) *n.* The box in which a dead body is buried.

collect (kə lekt´) *v.* To receive payment for a debt.

condescend (kon´ də send´) *v.* To act as if one is too good to do something.

condescending (kon´ də sen ding) *adj.* With an attitude of superiority.

conquer (kon´ kər) *v.* To overcome.

constantly (kän´ stənt lē) *adv.* All the time.

converge (kən vûrj´) *v.* To come together from different places.

core (kor) *n.* The central part of something.

corpse (korps) *n.* A dead body.

corral (kə ral´) *n.* A fenced-in area for cattle or horses.

country (kun´ trē) *n.* An area with fields and fewer houses than a city or town.

course (kors) *n.* A number of lessons given on a subject; a class.

crackerjack (krak´ ər jak´) *adj.* Extremely good.

creation (krē ā´ shən) *n.* Something that is made.

crimson (krim´ zən) *adj.* Deep red.

cultivate (kəl´ tə vāt´) *v.* To help plants grow better by breaking up the soil around them.

D

dainty (dān´ tē) *n.* A special, delicious food.—*adj.* Delicately beautiful.

deadbeat (ded´ bēt´) *n.* A person who owes money and doesn't pay.

debt (det) *n.* The condition of owing money.

decade (de´ kād´) *n.* A period of ten years.

decent (dē´ sənt) *adj.* Proper.

defenseless (di fense´ ləs) *adj.* Helpless.

delay (di lā´) *v.* To cause to wait.

delicious (di li´ shəs) *adj.* Pleasing to taste; tasty.

descendant (di sen´ dənt) *n.* A person's child or the child's child, and so on; anyone born from a particular family line.

detective (di tek´ tiv) *n.* A person who searches for information and gathers clues.

determined (di tûr´ mənd) *adj.* Firm and unwilling to change.

diamond (dī´ mənd) *n.* A valuable, clear-colored gem that sparkles in the light.

E

disappear (di′ sə pēr′) v. To vanish; to no longer be seen.

disappointed (di′ sə point′ əd) adj. Unhappy that something expected did not occur.

divider (di vī′ dər) n. Anything that cuts a thing into parts.

divvy (div′ ē) v. To divide for sharing.

donate (dō′ nāt) v. To give.

dorsal (dor′ səl) adj. On the upper side of the body; on the back.

dreadful (dred′ fəl) adj. Terrible; very bad.

drench (drench) v. To soak completely.

drift (drift) n. A mound formed by blowing wind.

drought (drout) n. Dry weather that lasts a very long time.

drowsily (drou′ zə lē) adv. Sleepily; in a sleepy way.

dugout (dug′ out′) n. A crude shelter made by digging a hole in the ground or on the side of a hill.

eager (ē′ gər) adj. Filled with excitement or interest.

earnings (ûr′ ningz) n. Money that is paid for doing a job.

ebb (eb) v. To flow away.

educational (e′ jə kā′ shnəl) adj. Helping one to gain knowledge or a skill.

elder (el′ dər) n. An official in certain churches.

elevated (el′ ə vā′ tid) adj. Raised up.

elevator (el′ ə vā′ tər) n. A building in which grain is handled and stored.

emblem (em′ bləm) n. A sign or figure that stands for something.

endure (en door′) v. To put up with; to bear.

equipment (i kwip′ mənt) n. Tools and supplies used for a given purpose.

errand (er′ ənd) n. A short trip to do something.

etch (ech) v. To outline clearly.

examine (ig za′ mən) v. To look at in detail.

exchange (iks chānj′) v. To trade one thing for another.

F

fail (fā´ əl) *v.* To lose worth.

fashion (fa´ shn) *n.* A style of clothing or jewelry that is popular at a given time. *adj.* To be in style.

feature (fē´ chər) *v.* To have in an important place.

fertile (fûr´ tl) *adj.* Fruitful; productive.

flamboyant (flam boi´ ənt) *adj.* Showy; bold; striking.

flavor (flā´ vər) *n.* Taste or specific quality.

folk (fōk) *n.* People or relatives; coming from or belonging to the common people.

folklore (fōk´ lor´) *n.* The legends, beliefs, and customs of a people.

forestry (for´ ə strē) *n.* The science of maintaining a forest.

formula (for´ myə lə) *n.* A set method for doing something.

forsaken (for sā´ kən) *v.* A past tense of **forsake:** To abandon; to give up.

foundation (foun dā´ shən) *n.* The base of a house.

frisky (fris´ kē) *adj.* Full of energy, playful, active.

frolic (frol´ ik) *n.* A party at which work is done. —*v.* To behave playfully.

frond (frond) *n.* A very large leaf.

frontlet (frənt´ lət) *n.* A carved wooden mask worn over the forehead as a part of a headdress, usually carved with the crest of the wearer.

fruit (frōot) *n.* Any kind of food that is grown and picked by hand.

furious (fyûr´ ē əs) *adj.* Violently angry.

G

gadget (ga´ jət) *n.* An invention for a special purpose.

garnet (gär´ nit) *n.* A deep red jewel.

generation (jen´ ə rā´ shən) *n.* A group of people who are about the same age.

girth (gûrth) *n.* A strap that goes around the body of a horse, usually to fasten a saddle.

glitch (glich) *n.* Something that doesn't work quite right.

gourd (gord) *n.* A melon-shaped fruit that can be dried, scooped out, and used as a bowl.

government (gə´ vərn mənt) *n.* The act or process of ruling a group of people.

grain (grān) *n.* A seed of corn, wheat, oats, rye, or other cereal plant.

graze (grāz) *v.* To eat grass.

Pronunciation Key: **at**; **l̄ate**; **c̄are**; **f̄ather**; **set**; **m̄e**; **it**; **k̄ite**; **ox**; **r̄ose**; **ô** in **b**ought; **coin**; **b͞o͞ok**; **t͞o͞o**; **form**; **out**; **up**; **ūse**; **tûrn**; **ə** sound in **a**bout, chick**e**n, penc**i**l, cann**o**n, circ**u**s; **chair**; **hw** in **wh**ich; **ri**ng; **sh**op; **th**in; **th**ere; **zh** in trea**s**ure.

grieve (grēv) *v.* To feel sadness because of loss or bad fortune.

griot (grē ō´) *n.* A person in a tribe whose job is to remember the oral history of all the families in the tribe or village.

gully (gu´ lē) *n.* A narrow ditch made by flowing water.

H

haltingly (hôl´ ting lē) *adv.* In a slow way.

handkerchief (hang´ kər chəf) *n.* A cloth used to wipe the nose or face.

harvest (här´ vəst) *v.* To bring the crops in from the field.

haul (hôl) *v.* To pull or move with force.

herd (hûrd) *n.* A group of animals.

hired (hī´ ərd) *adj.* Paid to work.

hitch (hich) *v.* To fasten with a loop or a hook.

holler (ho´ lər) *v.* To call out loudly.

hue (hū) *n.* A shade of color.

huppa (ho͞o´ pə) *n.* A covering that stands like a tent above the bride and groom in a Jewish wedding.

I

illustration (i´ ləs trā´ shən) *n.* A picture used to explain something written.

incite (in sīt´) *v.* To urge or bring to action.

inherit (in her´ it) *v.* To receive another person's property after his or her death.

inspect (in spekt´) *v.* To look at closely and carefully.

inspired (in spī´ ûrd) *adj.* Filled with a strong encouraging feeling.

install (in stôl´) *v.* To place a thing where it is going to be used.

invent (in vent´) *v.* To come up with a new idea for.

K

Klallam (klä´ lum) *n.* A coast Salish Indian tribe who live on a reservation called Little Boston, near Port Gamble, Washington.

L

ladle (lād´ l) *n.* A long-handled cup for serving liquids.

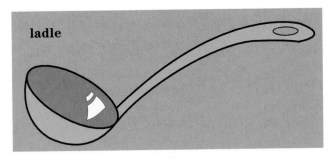

ladle

latex gum (lā´ teks gum´) *n.* A sticky liquid taken from a plant.

lather (la´ thər) *v.* To spread a foam made from soap and water over something.

launch (lônch) *v.* To get something started.

lean-to (lēn´ tōō´) *n.* A crude shelter with a sloping top that extends from a post or tree to the ground.

lease (lēs) *n.* An agreement to rent something.

legal (lē´ gəl) *adj.* Allowed by the rules or laws.

legend (le´ jənd) *n.* A story passed down that is not entirely true.

lingonberry (ling´ ən ber´ ē) *n.* A bright red berry related to the cranberry.

livelihood (liv´ lē hōod´) *n.* A way of making a living.

lox (loks) *n.* A form of salmon for eating.

lug (lug) *v.* To pull; to drag.

lump (lump) *n.* A piece; a chunk.

M

malfunction (mal´ fung´ shən) *v.* To break down or work badly.

mandarin (man´ də rən) *adj.* Orange or reddish-yellow.

mathematician (math´ ə mə tish´ ən) *n.* A person who works with numbers.

measurement (mezh´ ər mənt) *n.* The size of something.

memory (me mə rē) *n.* A thing or time remembered.

mend (mend) *v.* To fix or repair.

merchandise (mûr´ chən dīz) *n.* Items to be bought or sold.

merge (mûrj) *v.* To be mixed together.

message (me´ sij) *n.* A sign of what may be coming.

mode (mōd) *n.* A way.

model (mo´ dl) *v.* To wear in order to show others.

morsel (mor´ səl) *n.* A small piece of food.

mortgage (mor´ gij) *n.* The money borrowed to buy a house.

mosey (mō´ zē) *v.* To walk slowly; to stroll.

> **Pronunciation Key: at**; l**ā**te; c**â**re; f**ä**ther; s**e**t; m**ē**; **it**; k**ī**te; **ox**; r**ō**se; **ô** in b**ou**ght; c**oi**n; b**oo**k; t**oo**; f**o**rm; **ou**t; **up**; **ū**se; t**û**rn; **ə** sound in **a**bout, chick**e**n, penc**i**l, cann**o**n, circ**u**s; **ch**air; **hw** in **wh**ich; ri**ng**; **sh**op; **th**in; **th**ere; **zh** in trea**s**ure.

myth (mith) *n.* A story or legend from olden days that tries to explain something.

N

natural (na´ chə rəl) *n.* Not artificial or made by humans.

nestle (ne´ səl) *v.* To settle safely; to snuggle.

non-returnable (nän´ ri tûr´ nə bəl) *adj.* Something that cannot be taken or given back.

O

official (ə fi´ shəl) *adj.* Formal and proper.

operation (ä´ pə rā´ shən) *n.* An action performed with instruments on a living body to fix damage or improve health.

oral (or´ əl) *adj.* Spoken.

orchard (or´ chərd) *n.* An area containing fruit trees.

Ordnung (ord´ nəng) *n.* The Amish laws.

organdy (or´ gən dē) *n.* A smooth, stiff cotton material.

outwit (out´ wit´) *v.* To beat by being sly.

oval (ō´ vəl) *adj.* Egg-shaped.

overcome (ō´ vər kəm´) *v.* To beat or conquer.

P

padlock (pad´ lok´) *n.* A lock that can be taken off and put back on by unlocking a curved piece of metal.

parlor (pär´ lər) *n.* A somewhat private room used for business, conversation, entertaining, or receiving visitors.

partial (pär´ shəl) *adj.* Not complete.

pasture (pas´ chər) *n.* A field of grass in which cattle, horses, or sheep graze.

pattern (pat´ ərn) *n.* A model to follow when making clothes.

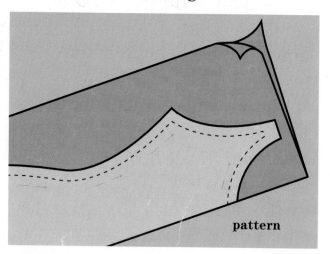

pattern

pesky (pes´ kē) *adj.* Causing trouble.

petunia (pi tōōn´ yə) *n.* A popular garden plant bearing funnel-shaped, colorful flowers.

pitch (pich) *n.* A dark, sticky substance used to make things waterproof.

pitifully (pit´ i flē) *adv.* Sadly.

pleasure (plezh´ ər) *v.* To please; to satisfy.

porcelain (por´ sə lin) *n.* A fine, delicate china.

portrait (por´ trət) *n.* A picture of someone.

positively (poz´ i tiv lē) *adv.* Certainly; for sure.

posse (pos´ ē) *n.* A group of people who gather to help a sheriff, usually on horses.

poverty (pov´ ər tē) *n.* The state of being poor.

prairie (prâr´ ē) *n.* Flat or rolling land covered with grass.

pretend (pri tend´) *v.* To make believe.

preserve (pri zûrv´) *v.* To keep safe.

profitable (prof´ i tə bəl) *adj.* Making money; gainful.

propose (prə pōz´) *v.* To offer a plan; to suggest.

pyramid (pēr´ ə mid´) *n.* An object with triangular sides that meet at a point at the top.

Q

quantity (kwän´ tə tē) *n.* A number or amount.

quote (kwōt) *v.* To state a price for something.

R

rampage (ram´ pāj) *v.* To act wild.

rawhide (rô´ hīd´) *n.* A piece of cattle hide, or skin, that has not been tanned, or turned into leather.

realty (rē´ əl tē) *n.* Property, including land and buildings; real estate.

recite (ri sīt´) *v.* To tell aloud.

reckon (rek´ ən) *v.* To think; to suppose.

recognize (re´ kig nīz´) *v.* To be aware that someone or something is familiar.

recollection (re´ kə lek´ shən) *n.* Something remembered; memories.

record (rek´ ərd) *n.* A piece of writing that tells a memory of some facts or events. —*v.* (ri kord´) To write down facts or information about events.

reflection (ri flek´ shən) *n.* An image or likeness seen in a surface such as water or glass.

reign (rān) *v.* To rule.

rein (rān) *n.* A strap used for control by a rider of a horse or the driver of a carriage.

rein in (rān´ in´) *v.* To stop a horse by pulling the reins.

relative (re´ lə tiv) *n.* A person who is related by either blood or marriage to another.

relieve (ri lēv´) *v.* To comfort.

reluctantly (ri luk´ tənt lē) *adv.* Not willingly.

remain (ri mān) *v.* To stay the same or to stay in the same place.

rent (rent) *v.* To provide the use of something for a fee; to pay a fee in order to use something.

repeat (ri pēt´) *n.* Something that is done again.

replenish (ri ple´ nish) *v.* Fill up again.

rescue (res´ kū) *v.* To save or free.

reservation (re zər vā´ shən) *n.* 1. Public land set aside for the use of Native American tribes. 2. Something that is kept back or withheld.

reserve (ri zûrv´) *v.* To set aside for later use.

rolling pin (rō´ ling pin´) *n.* A cylinder with handles, used to roll dough flat.

rotation (rō tā´ shən) *n.* Taking turns planting different crops in different years on the same land.

route (rōōt) *n.* A road or path.

S

saddle (sa´ dəl) *n.* A leather seat for riding a horse.

safekeeping (sāf´ kē´ ping) *n.* The act of protecting something.

sagebrush (sāj´ brush´) *n.* A grayish-green shrub that grows in the dry West.

scarcely (skârs´ lē) *adv.* Barely.

scurry (skûr´ ē) *v.* To move quickly as if in a great hurry.

seasonal (sē´ zə nl) *adj.* Ripe at a certain time of the year.

seedling (sēd´ ling) *n.* A very young plant.

sensible (sen´ sə bəl) *adj.* Having or showing good sense.

serial (sēr´ ē əl) *adj.* Arranged in a sequence or series.

sharecropper (shâr´ krä´ pər) *n.* A person who farms someone else's land and is paid with a share of the crops.

shear (shēr) *v.* To clip; to cut.

shun (shun) *v.* To keep away from.

silage (sī´ lij) *n.* Feed for farm animals.

silo (sī´ lō) *n.* A tall building for storing food for animals on a farm.

skillet (skil´ it) *n.* A frying pan.

software (sôft´ wâr´) *n.* Written programs and data used to operate a computer.

sow (sou) *n.* An adult female pig.

spade (spād) *n.* A digging tool with a flat blade and a long handle.

speaker stick (spē´ kər stik) *n.* A long, straight pole that is carved with the crest of the chief and shows that he is the leader of the tribe. When the chief holds it, the people listen to his words of advice or wisdom.

splendid (splen´ dəd) *adj.* Magnificent; glorious.

sprawl (sprôl) *v.* To spread out.

spread (spred) *v.* To stretch out in different directions.

station (stā´ shən) *n.* A place where a service is performed.

string (string) *v.* To stretch from one place to another.

strongbox (strông´ boks´) *n.* A sturdy box with a lock for holding money or other valuable items.

suction (suk´ shən) *n.* A pulling force that uses a sucking action.

support (sə port´) *v.* To provide all the money needed.

surplus (sûr´ plus) *n.* An amount more than is needed; an extra amount.

suspicion (sə spish´ ən) *n.* An idea that something is wrong, but without proof.

swift (swift) *adj.* Able to move quickly.

symbol (sim´ bəl) *n.* Something that represents or stands for something else.

T

tailor (tā´ lər) *n.* A person who makes clothing.

tatter (tat´ ər) *v.* To tear.

teeming (tē´ ming) *adj.* Swarming; filled with.

tempting (temp´ ting) *adj.* Attractive; desirable.

tender (ten´ dər) *n.* Money, payment.

terrapin (ter´ ə pin) *n.* A type of turtle.

thrive (thrīv) *v.* To survive; to do well.

tinker (ting´ kər) *v.* To repair in a clumsy or makeshift way; to putter.

toil (toil) *v.* To work hard.

token (tō´ kən) *n.* A piece of metal shaped like a coin, used instead of money.

totem (tō´ təm) *n.* An animal or object from which a family traces its clan origins.

totem pole (tō´ təm pōl) *n.* A tall pole carved from a single log with a design showing several **totems** stacked one upon the other. Totem poles are made to honor an individual or to tell a legend or story.

tractor (trak´ tər) *n.* A farm vehicle that can pull wagons, plows, or other farming equipment.

tradition (trə dish´ ən) *n.* A custom handed down through many generations; the handing down of customs or beliefs from one generation to another.

tranquil (tran´ kwəl) *adj.* Calm and quiet.

traveller (tra´ və lər) *n.* A person who goes on a trip or a journey.

treasure (tre´ zhər) *n.* Something valuable.

treasured (trezh´ ərd) *adj.* Regarded as being of great value.

tribe (trīb) *n.* A group of persons or clans with one common language and living under a leader or chief.

trickster (trik´ stər) *n.* A character or person who delights in playing tricks on others and is skilled at doing so. In the **Tsimshian** stories, Raven was a well-known trickster.

trillion (tril´ yən) *n.* The number 1,000,000,000,000; a very large number.

trinket (trin´ kət) *n.* A small ornament.

Tsimshian (tsim´ shē an) *n.* A tribe of Northwest Coast Indians who came from the banks of the Nass and Skeena Rivers of British Columbia.

turpentine

turpentine (tûr´ pən tīn´) *n.* An oil used to thin paint.

twirl (twûrl) *v.* To spin around.

U

udder (ud´ ər) *n.* The part of a cow's body from which it gives milk.

unharness (un här´ nis) *v.* To take off the leather straps that fasten a horse to a buggy.

unpredictable (un´ pri dik´ tə bəl) *adj.* Not able to be planned; not certain.

unite (ū nīt´) *v.* To work together as a group.

untangle (un tang´ gəl) *v.* To remove tangles or knots.

V

vanish (van´ ish) *v.* To disappear.

vital (vīt´ l) *adj.* Necessary.

volunteer (vol´ ən tēr´) *v.* To offer to do something.

yam

W

weaver (wē´ vər) *n.* A person who makes fabric from thread or yarn.

weigh (wā) *v.* To measure how heavy something is.

whinny (hwi´ nē) *n.* A sound made by a horse.

widow (wid´ ō) *n.* A woman whose husband has died.

willies (wil´ ēz) *n. pl.* A nervous fear.

wilt (wilt) *v.* To droop; to fade.

workbench (wûrk´ bench´) *n.* A strong table used for working with tools and materials.

wound (wound) *v.* Past tense of **wind**: To wrap around and around.

Y

yam (yam) *n.* A type of sweet potato.

Photo Credits